D0970737

THE
1 HOUR
CHINA
BOOK
(2017 Edition)

TWO PEKING UNIVERSITY PROFESSORS EXPLAIN ALL OF CHINA BUSINESS IN SIX SHORT STORIES

JEFFREY TOWSON
JONATHAN WOETZEL

This publication is designed to provide accurate information in regard to the subject matter covered. It is sold with the understanding that the publisher is not engaged in rendering professional services.

ISBN-10: 0991445023 (paperback)
ISBN-13: 978-0-9914450-2-8 (paperback)

Version 2016.12.16

10 9 8 7 6 5 4 3 2 1

CONTENTS

PREFACE TO THE 2017 EDITION..V

CAN YOU EXPLAIN CHINA IN AN HOUR?...1

MEGA-TREND #1: URBANIZATION..13

MEGA-TREND #2: HUGE MANUFACTURING SCALE.......................39

MEGA-TREND #3: RISING CHINESE CONSUMERS.........................59

MEGA-TREND #4: MONEY – AND LOTS OF IT.................................80

MEGA-TREND #5: THE BRAINPOWER BEHEMOTH........................101

MEGA-TREND #6: THE CHINESE INTERNET..................................124

FINAL THOUGHTS..140

ALSO BY THE AUTHORS

One Hour China Consumer Book: Five Short Stories That Explain the Brutal Fight for One Billion Consumers, by Jeffrey Towson and Jonathan Woetzel (May 2015)

No Ordinary Disruption: The Four Global Forces Breaking All the Trends, by Jonathan Woetzel, James Manyika, Richard Dobbs (May, 2015)

What Would Ben Graham Do Now? A New Value Investing Playbook for a Global Age, by Jeffrey Towson (May 21, 2011)

Operation China: From Strategy to Execution, by Jimmy Hexter and Jonathan Woetzel (December 18, 2007)

Capitalist China: Strategies for a Revolutionized Economy, by Jonathan Woetzel (August 13, 2003)

PREFACE
TO THE
2017 EDITION

It has been three years since we published the *One Hour China* book. And three years is a really long time in China. For example, in this three year period:

- Over 30 million people moved into Chinese cities. By 2025, China will have ten New York-sized cities.

- 60 million people bought cars and over a thousand miles of metro lines (the distance from Dallas to Chicago) were built.

- Over 20 million people graduated from Chinese universities. Also during this period, China sent more than 1.4 million students to study overseas.

- Over 360 million Chinese tourists traveled out of the country.

- Chinese companies made over $400 billion in overseas acquisitions.

- China's foreign exchange reserves first grew by $800 billion and then shrank by $1 trillion to wind up at around $3 trillion.

Things move pretty fast in the PRC. We thought an updated edition of this book was definitely needed.

We also thought it was important to check how our main thesis has held up. We have argued that six mega-trends (urbanization, manufacturing, consumers, brainpower, capital and the Internet) drive most of China business. And that these trends explain most of the China stories you see in the news. We are pleased to see our thesis has held up over time.

However, in some cases, these mega-trends have begun growing even faster. For example, Chinese consumers are now a global force. Back in 2013, sales on the November 11 singles' day holiday (in Chinese this translates to "me me me me") outsold American Cyber Monday by 3:1. This ratio has now climbed to 5:1, with over $17 billion transacted in one day. McKinsey & Company has recently forecast that the working Chinese consumer will account for over a third of global consumption growth through 2030.

The intersection of the consumption and manufacturing trends is also becoming interesting. For example, technology's richest woman globally is now Hong Kong-based Zhou Qunfei. Born in a poor, rural community in mainland China, Zhou was a factory worker in the glass industry before starting her own company, Lens Technology. Today, Lens Technology is one of the world's largest manufacturers of screens for mobile phones and tablets (and Chinese consumers are the biggest buyers of smartphones). Lens Technology went public in March 2015 and Qunfei now has an estimated net worth of $6.4 billion.

We found that the Internet chapter did need a serious update. This is not surprising as the Chinese Internet, and smartphones in particular, moves at a startling speed. It is also pretty unpredictable. As we are writing this, Chinese company Meitu is preparing for a Hong Kong IPO. Meitu offers a mobile photo editing application that lets you alter your appearance in your photos – such as by making your chin narrower, your eyes bigger, and so on. In the past two years, Chinese women have began using this app to "beautify" their selfies in stunning numbers. Over 440M Chinese women are now using the application. "Beautifying selfies" was a market virtually nobody saw coming. Even the CEO of Meitu has said it was a total surprise. These kinds of surprises are fairly common in the Chinese Internet.

Note: in September 2016, a woman was pulled over for drunk driving in Western Xinjiang. After a breathalyzer confirmed intoxication, the police began taking photos for evidence. The woman then demanded that they use Meitu for their photos, so she would look better.

***

We wrote the *One Hour China* book for "smart but busy people". We wrote it for people who wanted to know more about China business but who were not going to live in China. And who really didn't have time to read 10-15 weighty books on China. We wrote this book based on what we would say to a smart but busy person if they gave us one hour of their time.

That turned out to be a pretty good idea. The book went to the top of the Amazon best-seller list (for China) and stayed there for over two years. It is now also being taught in business schools, foreign policy programs and and undergraduate programs around the world. One reviewer described it as a "minor publishing sensation", which we thought was a pretty apt summary for such a little book.

We hope this book helps you understand China a bit more. China's impact on global markets is continuing to grow. This book is probably more relevant today than when we first wrote it. We are really just at the beginning of this phenomenon.

Thanks again for reading,
Jeff and Jonathan.
January 2017

CAN YOU EXPLAIN CHINA IN AN HOUR?

China is big.

That's our attention-grabbing opening. China is really, really big. It's important to be provocative in publishing.

China is also really complicated. By economy, by industry, by population and by just about every other metric, the country keeps getting more and more complicated. China is now both really big and really complicated – not unlike, say, the United States and Europe.

So the idea of a one-hour China book is kind of ridiculous. How could you possibly explain such a big and sprawling topic in an hour?

But it's not actually a theoretical question. We both do "China-to-the-world" thinking for a living. And more and more, we have found ourselves getting asked about China in places like Ohio, Brighton and Lima. Places that five years ago didn't really care that much about this topic.

And the questions are not just coming from business people now. They are also coming from academics, concerned parents, policymakers and many other groups. China has become an important topic most everywhere. But most people don't have the time to read lots of weighty China books. Some prominent American politicians know shockingly little about China by the way.

So this book is our answer to this situation. If we had the undivided attention of someone from Ohio, Brighton or Lima for just one hour, this little book is what we would say.

And we took it a bit farther. Not only is this book our one-hour explanation of China business, it is also written so that it can be read once, thrown away (please don't) and remembered easily. That was our goal: **a speed-read China book that explains most things and sticks in the brain.**

If we have done our job well, you should be able to read this in 60-90 minutes. You can read the main points in an hour. If you read absolutely everything, it will take closer to 90 minutes. And after one reading, you should have a reliable framework for understanding China business. Most China headlines (say in the Wall Street Journal) should make sense. In fact, they should be fairly predictable.

ABOUT US: THE VIEW FROM THE LAOWAI TRENCHES

We both live and work with one foot in China and one foot out. We do China-to-the-world thinking for a living. Our main careers are in management consulting (Jonathan) and private equity deals / advisory (Jeff). But we also write and teach at business schools.

Jonathan is a senior partner at McKinsey & Company in Shanghai and is co-Director of the McKinsey Global Institute. And he was the guy that opened their Shanghai office in 1994. If you want to know the answer to a ridiculously specific question like "what was Baosteel working on in 1995?", Jonathan probably knows the answer. And there is a good chance that he was part of the team answering it. Jeff refers to him as the "national archive for China business".

Jonathan Woetzel

Jeff is an investor and advisor focused on US-China private equity deals. Jeff's background was shaped by eight years working as an executive / slave to Prince Alwaleed. Alwaleed is usually known as the Saudi Prince who bought Citibank, News Corp and the Four Seasons. He is also occasionally known as the guy building the one-mile skyscraper in Jeddah (Jeff's old project.) and the Prince who turned an Airbus A380 into a private plane.

Jeffrey Towson

We both work in the trenches of China business. We spend our days digging into companies and industries. We are bottom-up analysts and our view of the world is based on studying and working with thousands of individual companies. Jonathan is also known for his ability to speak Mandarin so fluently that it shocks Chinese. Jeff has an accent that produces much the same effect.

As professors, our academic home is Peking University's Guanghua School of Management in Beijing. Although it desperately needs a Starbucks, it is otherwise a great place to teach. Our students have come from virtually every-where: China, South Korea, Singapore, Norway, Los Angeles, New York, Azerbaijan, Egypt, Germany and so on. Generally speaking, they are crazy ambitious, which we respect. It is completely normal for MBA courses in China to run until 10pm on Friday night.

An important note: Some of our 2012 MBA students were involved in the first edition of this book. We have highlighted them at the end of this chapter.

THE ONLY 6 STORIES YOU NEED TO KNOW TO UNDERSTAND CHINA

A lot of China business can appear to have a mysterious quality. It can seem strange and far away. This is not uncommon for new industries or markets. Our first assertion is to relax. There is nothing mysterious or terribly difficult about Chinese companies or markets. In business, there is really nothing new under the sun. Consumers behave pretty much the same everywhere. Competition is pretty much the same everywhere. You just need to ignore the hype and hyperbole and stay focused on the basics.

And in China today, the basics are 6 big trends.

That's it. There are six big trends that shape most of the industries. These six trends are also driving much of China's impact on the world. They are like tectonic plates moving underneath the surface. If you can understand them, the chaotic flurry of activity on the surface becomes a lot more understandable – and even predictable.

However, we are talking about trends that move businesses on a monthly basis. These are revenue or cost drivers that you can see in income statements. That is different than the high-level, "trends" that are typically discussed by economists, politicians and other macro analysts. Our trends are phenomena that are generating revenue, creating big companies and minting Chinese millionaires (and billionaires).

You will probably notice that we have little to say about Chinese politics or state capitalism. For some reason, Western business people who normally study customers and competitors shift their focus to politics and regulations when in China. Our experience is that these topics are wildly over-emphasized by Westerners in China. The business of China is mostly business.

Our big assertion is that six mega-trends are driving most of China's business today – and its interaction with the rest of the world. The deals, the newspaper headlines, and the rising and falling wealth of companies are mostly manifestations of these six mega-trends – which we show below.

The 6 China Megatrends

The brainpower behemoth

The Chinese Internet

Rising Chinese consumers

Money - and lots of it

Urbanization

Manufacturing scale

This is our simple framework. If you remember one thing from this book, it should be this chart. We will repeatedly come back to it throughout the book. In each of the following chapters, we will be talking about one of these six mega-trends. And we will be telling a story for each. We will tell the stories of six individuals that rode these trends to staggering wealth.

So you can look at business in China as either six mega-trends or as six short stories, depending on how your brain works. And this is our basic proposition. **You give us 60-90 minutes and we will give you six stories and a chart that explain most of China business.**

However, let us make an important caveat. These are powerful trends that are driving business activity today. It does not mean they are necessarily good things. Or that they are stable or sustainable. Most lead to profits, or at least revenue. Some may be stable. But some lead to bubbles that may or may not collapse. We are only arguing that they are big and are driving economic activity on a very large scale.

OUR THANKS FOR READING OUR BOOK

This book is the result of the expertise of +30 people - including MBAs, McKinsey partners, China writers and many editors. While small, it represents a lot of expertise that we have tried to distill down to a speed-read that sticks in the brain.

We hope that our enthusiasm for this topic also comes across. The rise of China and its increasing collision with the world is a fascinating topic. And it is something we live on a daily basis. It's a fascinating life. Dynamic. Fairly chaotic. Often anxious. May you live in interesting times...

Our thanks for reading our little (literally) book. We hope you find it helpful or at least a good way to kill a taxi ride home. We tried to keep it to one hour (and the price of a latte).

Also, if you would like to receive other reading recommendations, please sign up at www.onehourchina.com. The follow-up to this book, the One Hour China Consumer Book, is also now available.

Our thanks and cheers,
Jonathan and Jeff

***

MBAS YOU SHOULD HAVE ON YOUR RADAR

Please take a moment to look at the 2012 MBAs who have worked on this project.

CHAPTER ON URBANIZATION:

Edan Kaplansky. Born in Manhattan and raised in Jerusalem, Edan holds an L.L.B. and an M.B.A. from Hebrew University, with studies at Peking University's Guanghua School of Management. After his

MBA, he worked at Shibolet and Co., Advocates & Notaries, and was Managing Director of the 'Brera Center' Foundation, which provides free legal and educational services to underprivileged populations.

Ron Klein. Born in Chicago and raised in Israel, Ron holds an L.L.B. from Hebrew University Faculty of Law, where he served as Deputy-Editor of the Faculty Law Review. He also holds an M.B.A. from Hebrew University and Peking University, majoring in International Finance. After graduation, Ron worked at the Israeli Securities Authority, focusing on Corporate Governance and Securities Regulation Policy.

Wang Xinran holds an M.B.A. from Peking University and focuses on business operations and strategic management. After graduatoin, Xinran worked for SMIC (Semiconductor Manufacturing International Corporation) as an investment manager.

Yinan Zhang. Yinan focused on Strategy and Investment at Peking University. Prior to attending business school, Yinan worked for several multinational firms including Kraft Foods, Unilever and Nestle, focusing on supply chain management. Yinan earned a Bachelor's degree in engineering from Beijing Normal University in 2005.

CHAPTER ON RISING CHINESE CONSUMERS:

Scott Hicks. Scott earned his MBA at the University of British Columbia, where he specialized in Finance, Strategic Management, and International Business. Holding a CFA charter, he has worked for the Canadian Federal Government and in the treasury department of Finning International.

Denis Lenz holds a Bachelor's degree in Business Administration from the University of St. Gallen, Switzerland. Born and raised in

China, he has strong international exposure and a great interest in Asia's dynamic societies.

CHAPTER ON MANUFACTURING:

Christopher L. Amador was a 2013 candidate in the Master of International Affairs program at the University of St. Gallen in Switzerland. He has experience in the automotive and consulting industry through internships with BMW Group and Bain & Company, where he worked on China-related topics.

Jangyoon (Johnny) Kim. A native of Seoul, Korea, Johnny is an established consultant and project manager. He is intrigued by China's potential to shape the global economic landscape.

Maria Elena Kolesch earned her Bachelor of Science in Business Administration from Germany's leading business university, Mannheim, in 2011. She completed her Master's in Corporate Management and Economics at Germany's "Zeppelin University."

CHAPTER ON FINANCIAL SERVICES:

Juuso Makinen is an economics major from Helsinki intrigued by the challenges of emerging markets – particularly financial liberalization and asset pricing issues. As a student at Peking University, he gained insights into social and economic topics pertaining to China.

James Liu

Kexin Zheng was a part-time M.B.A. student at Peking University's Guanghua School of Management. She holds a Bachelor's degree in Economics and Sociology from Peking University. She served as a credit analyst at MetLife China and previously worked as a banking analyst at CCXI, the largest local credit rating company in China.

CHAPTER ON BRAINPOWER:

Theresa Gessner. With a background in corporate communications and management studies, her field of interest lies in cross-cultural management and international communication strategy. She earned her MSc from Stockholm University in 2013.

Spence Nichol was an associate with a global management consultancy, and a former strategic advisor to one of the world's best performing school systems. He has studied at London Business School, the China-Europe International Business School in Shanghai, and the University of Alberta in his native Canada.

Xiaoyi (Fenny) Wang. A senior software engineer, Fenny has been working in a multinational telecom company for over eight years. She graduated from the University of Toronto with a Bachelor's degree in Computer Science, and later studied in Peking University's MBA program.

CHAPTER ON THE INTERNET:

Peter Lehmann is a digital business professional with German roots and a global mindset. By following market trajectories and technology trends, he aims to build the products and services of the future. The insights he contributed to this book are the result of his studies at Peking University.

Stephan Maluck. Born 1986 in Germany, Stephan studied Management at universities in Germany, China, and Chile. He holds a Master's degree and works as a management consultant in the financial services industry while pursuing his Ph.D. Prior to graduate school, Mr. Maluck completed an apprenticeship at Deutsche Bank and developed an entrepreneurial mind-set as an executive assistant of a German start-up.

Mathis Wilke holds an M.B.A. from CEIBS in Shanghai. During his studies he won the China Final of the CFA Institute Research Competition in Shanghai, and placed as a Semi-Finalist at the Asia-Pacific Regional Final in Hong Kong. Prior to business school, he worked as a Senior Associate in the Leveraged Finance departments of RBS and Mediobanca for five years, financing private equity transactions across Europe. He speaks German, English, Spanish and Mandarin Chinese.

Janet Yurasova. Originally from Russia, Janet graduated with an M.B.A. from the UCLA Anderson School of Management. Before attending Anderson, she ran a small web-development company and started three successful Internet endeavors. Janet has a diverse educational background in business, IT, law and social sciences from US, Russian, French, Cyprus and Chinese universities.

GENERAL RESEARCH:

Stian André Kvig holds an MSc. from Copenhagen Business School. Mr. Kvig has held several internships involving international capital markets during his studies, and he manages a private portfolio of investments. He has working proficiency in German and conversational ability in Mandarin.

Also thanks to Luke Masuda for his help with this project. Finally, a special thanks to Glenn Leibowitz of McKinsey. We are both greatly appreciative of his invaluable support and his generosity with his time.

MEGA-TREND #1:
URBANIZATION

China is currently witnessing the largest migration in human history. Hundreds of millions of people are flooding from the countryside into the cities. And while over 300 million people have already migrated in the past 30 years, McKinsey predicts there are another 350 million yet on the way.

China's urban population (M) over time

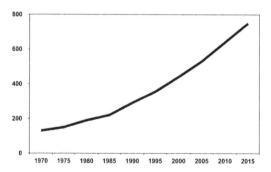

Source: China Statistical Yearbook

This urbanization phenomenon is adding an average of 18.5 million people to China's cities every year. That is equivalent to adding the population of the Netherlands annually. Or the equivalent of adding the entire population of Japan every 8 years.

This process began in earnest in the 1980s when government controls on where people could live were loosened (to some degree). Prior to this, the Chinese population had been somewhat frozen in place. For example, in 1980, only 20 percent of the Chinese population was located in cities. In the US in 1980, it was 70 percent. So this massive urbanization process is a lot about China catching up. It is about transitioning from an agricultural to an urban industrial society.

Such a huge migration of people changes almost everything: cities, required infrastructure, environmental impact, required resources, the economy, etc. As cities contain virtually every aspect of life, such a migration changes virtually everything in China. However, this is not just an economic and demographic trend (which we will discuss). It is also a cultural phenomenon.

For many Chinese, the move from their home village to the city is a key moment in their lives. Workers, young college graduates and even entire families have strong memories of leaving their village for the first time and taking the train ride to Shenzhen or Shanghai. As in America's great migration West in the 1800's, this movement into the cities represents the search for opportunity and a better life.

On national holidays, workers return to their villages from the cities. Rain delays during these periods can cause massive congestion - as in the Guangzhou railway station in January 2008 (photo: Tan Qingiu / ChinaFotoPress)

Urbanization is our first China mega-trend. We have placed it as the starting point in our chart (below) - as it is the most important phenomenon shaping modern China. We will make just a few key points about this trend (helpfully noted as Key Points) and then we will tell a short story about its impact. This will be our process for each chapter - one story and a few Key Points.

The 6 China Megatrends

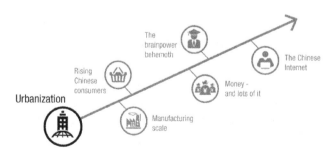

KEY POINT #1: THERE WILL SOON BE 1 BILLION CHINESE CITY DWELLERS

From 1980 to 2015, China's urban population grew by approximately 450 million. That is more than the entire population of the USA. This brought the number of Chinese city-dwellers to about 750 million and the overall urbanization rate to 55 percent. However, this is still far below the 70-80 percent urbanization rate seen in Japan, the US and Europe. So we still have a long way to go.

In 2009, the McKinsey Global Institute (and Jonathan specifically) published a widely cited report, "Preparing for China's Urban Billion." It showed how by 2030, there will be over 1 billion Chinese city dwellers. That's the number to remember: 1 billion city dwellers. Chinese urbanization is increasing at a fairly linear rate toward this big milestone.

When this happens, China's cities will be more populous than the North and South American continents combined. The implications of this are profound. And 1 billion is a good number to keep in mind. It's also pretty easy to remember.

KEY POINT #2: LOTS OF CITY DWELLERS MEANS LOTS OF CITIES

Not a big surprise. All these people moving into the cities have to live somewhere. So they need apartments. And they need buses and subways to get to work. And they need water and electricity. And then they need things like police, parks, roads and sewage treatment. These are not little challenges.

Obviously, a lot of Chinese cities just got bigger in response. Most added new districts. We can today count 160 Chinese cities with over 1 million people. In comparison, Europe has 35. And McKinsey predicts this number will increase to about 220 by 2025. So think 220 cities like Tucson, Arizona.

Some cities got a lot bigger. China currently has 16 cities with over 5 million people - and this will increase to 23 by 2025. So think 23 San Francisco's (a scary thought for conservative America). And these will constitute 40 percent of the world's cities with over 5 million people.

And finally, we are seeing the emergence of mega-cities. These cities, usually several cities linked closely together, contain 30-40 million people each. And many will reach 50-60 million people. These are fascinating and we will discuss them more in the key point on clusters.

Our point here is that there is a ton of building going on to handle the inflow of people. And it is not something that any country has ever attempted before. It also occasionally produces some unusual situations. An example is Shenzhen, often called a "city without memory".

***

Shenzhen is today, by any definition, a world-class, first-tier city. Located directly across the border from Hong Kong, it has several modern business districts, great parks, more than 10 million people, and a subway system that has grown from nothing to very large in about 10 years.

It is also a "city without memory". It is a place where you always ask where someone is from, because nobody is from Shenzhen. The city was only a series of villages prior to 1980. The total population then was about 100,000. And as recently as 1995, the central business district Futian was empty fields. Building a thriving city from scratch in just over two decades is an impressive feat with some strange consequences.

Shenzhen today (photo: Chumash Maxim / Shutterstock)

If Shenzhen is a city without memory, Kangbashi in Inner Mongolia is often called a "ghost city", another unusual situation created by urbanization. Mostly empty Kangbashi was built from scratch for an anticipated 1 million inhabitants by 2023. This population, by and large, did not show up and projections have been reduced to 300,000. So today it's a big, impressive and empty city. There are communities of empty apartment blocks. Modern government buildings and retail spaces are deserted. Kangbashi and other ghost cities get a lot of media attention – especially when discussing China's real estate bubbles.

Our point is that all of this is to be expected. If you are building cities at a breakneck pace against a huge urbanization inflow, sometimes your supply gets ahead of your demand. That, plus some real estate speculation and debt, gets you a ghost city. And sometimes your demand gets ahead of your supply and you get congestion (e.g., crowded Beijing). And sometimes you get it about right (e.g., Shenzhen). These things should be expected and are not as significant as newspaper headlines would have you believe.

KEY POINT #3: IN CHINA, URBANIZATION = WEALTH

Human beings are social animals. Putting us in close proximity to each other, such as in cities, changes us. And urbanization is fundamentally changing the Chinese people. How they act. How they shop. How they communicate. It is also changing their economic status.

In China, urbanization equals wealth. Going city-by-city across China, urbanization has directly coincided with approximately 350 million Chinese moving out of poverty since 1990. GDP per capita just goes up faster in cities.

And not only have 250 Chinese cities tripled their GDP per capita since 1990, but disposable income per capita is also up over 300%. So what you are seeing in Chinese cities is both an increase in the number of people in cities and an increase in spending power per person.

Facing massive urbanization, cities can easily vary between over-capacity (i.e., ghost cities) and congestion - as in the city of Shanghai (above)
(© chuyu/123RF Stock Photo)

This is not necessarily a causal relationship. And in most countries, urbanization does not directly lead to wealth (hello Latin America). More likely urbanization is necessary for wealth, even if by itself it is not sufficient. We make no claim for why this is happening in China. But the data is overwhelming. Note the chart below.

Chinese urbanization (%) vs. GDP / capita (RMB)

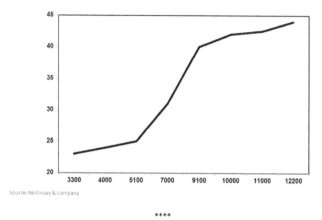

Source: McKinsey & Company

****

That's the end of the numbers for this chapter. Some people relate better to numbers (Jeff wants his obituary to be a PowerPoint presentation). But most people relate better to stories. And for Chinese urbanization, a good story to remember is that of Wang Shi and his company, China Vanke.

THE AWESOME STORY OF WANG SHI AND CHINA VANKE

China Vanke is a real estate company that has no equivalent in the West. The company's revenues are greater than the top four American real estate developers combined. It has built more apartments than any other company in history. And Wang Shi, the founder, is now the world's largest real estate developer. He is also the person who has provided a defining event for millions of rising Chinese: the purchase of their first home.

China Vanke is strictly a residential real estate developer. They make simple, clean apartments for China's middle class. That's it. This is a simple "value for money" proposition, which is a very common strategy among China's first moguls. He did not really innovate. He did not offer luxury. He offered basic quality homes at a affordable price. And he did it in great volume very quickly. For example, in 2015 alone, China Vanke sold over 20 million square million in apartments across more than 25 Chinese cities.

Wang Shi, Chairman of China Vanke (Photo: Imaginechina)

A PRETTY INSPIRING RAGS-TO-RICHES STORY

Wang Shi was born in 1951 in a military family in Liu-zhou, Guangxi. Even today, this is a world away from Shanghai and Beijing. But back in the 1950s, it was deep in the wilderness of China. It was an isolated and poor city that was just recovering from its occupation by Japan in World War II.

Shi graduated from junior high school in 1968 at the height of the Cultural Revolution, a time when urban youth and other groups were being relocated to the coun-tryside. Coming of age during this difficult period of Chi-na's history is a common theme for many of the successful business people we will discuss in this book.

Following his parents' advice, Shi joined the army and headed off to Xuzhou, Jiangsu (near Shanghai). However after just 6 months, he was transferred to the Turpan Basin in Xinjiang. This is just about as far northwest as you can go in China. It was literally the end of the world at that time. And for 5 years, Shi worked there within a military logistics group. Finally in 1973, he left the army and found a job as a furnace worker in the Zhengzhou Railway Bureau in Henan in central China.

The now 23-year-old Shi eventually enrolled in the Department of Water Supply and Drainage Engineering at the Lanzhou College of Transportation, capturing one of the only two entrance opportunities available. After graduation, he returned to southern China and began work in the engineering section of the Guangzhou Rail-way Bureau

In terms of rags to super riches stories, it is difficult to find a more humble beginning for a billionaire than Wang Shi's story. To come of age in rural China during the Cultural Revolution meant a focus on survival. And Shi's early movements between colleges, military positions and government jobs were not uncommon. These were largely the only career options available in China at that time.

By 27, Shi had settled down. He worked on several civil engineering projects as a technician, got married to Wang Jianghui, the daughter of a retired deputy party secretary of Guangdong Province, and started a family. There was virtually no indication of the capitalist heights to which he would soon rise.

However, in 1980, Shi took and passed the recruitment examination for the Department of Foreign Trade and Economic Cooperation of Guangdong Province. This would turn out to be the move that would change everything for him. For Guangdong, just across the border from Hong Kong, was about to become the first part of China to open to the world. Another common theme of the success stories in this book is being in Guangdong and Shenzhen in the early 1980s.

Shi became a liaison for Guangdong's Foreign Trade and Economic Relationship Committee. Whether by strategy or luck, he had found himself in the epicenter of newly capitalist China. As China opened to the world, foreign trade through Shenzhen and Guangdong was the first big economic activity. And as liaison for the foreign trade committee, he likely had a bird's eye view into the business opportunities being created at that time.

In 1983, Shi quit his job and struck out on his own. He went right to Shenzhen, which had by that time been designated China's first Special Economic Zone. He was not alone in this move. Government officials from all over China were jumping into business and heading to Shenzhen. But as mentioned, while Shenzhen is a first tier city today, it was not much more than a series of villages in the early 1980s.

Shi struck gold fairly quickly. At that time, China needed basically everything and those bringing goods across the Shenzhen border were extracting large profits. Shi made his first 3 million renminbi (about US$1 million at that time) by bringing in corn and reselling it to an animal feed company. He used this first windfall to jump into consumer electronics, importing electronic equipment from Japan and then selling them to the local market. He also started up several manufacturing plants for garments, watches, beverages and printing. Shenzhen had become a boomtown for just about every type of product. Shi would later say, "Except for pornography, gambling, drugs, and weapons, Vanke (his company) did almost everything." His company Vanke, in Chinese, basically means diversification.

What Shi was doing was deal-making. He was trading, buying and selling – basically cutting deals amid the frenzy of China's opening to the world. According to China Daily, he was at one point the biggest importer in Shenzhen.

However, this chapter is about the urbanization mega-trend. And while Shi was successful, so were many others. He had not yet caught the mega-trend that would rocket him upwards above the rest.

That changed in November 1988 when Shi participated in a land auction for the first time. He made an astonishingly high bid for the "Vuitton Villa" land plot in Shenzhen. His bid was so high it surprised everyone, including the auction officer. But it got him into the real estate game. And with his first real estate project acquired, his company began to transform from a trading house (called the "Modern Educational Equipment Exhibit Center") into a real estate developer. He also raised 28 million renminbi in funds (about US$7.6 million at that time).

From there, his rise was meteoric. The massive migration of Chinese into cities - as well as the movement of current urban residents into nicer apartments - created a huge demand for modern residential housing. In 1991, just three years after its first real estate deal, China Vanke went public on the Shenzhen Stock Exchange. It was the second company to list on the new exchange.

As mentioned, China Vanke focused on basic residential units for the middle class. And they turned them out in great numbers. China Vanke quickly became the largest residential real estate developer in China, with operating income and net profits growing annually at approximately 30 percent and 35 percent.

China Vanke builds the modern apartments that China's rising middle class is upgrading to (© Ping Han/123RF Stock Photo)

In 2015, China Vanke's annual sales exceeded 260 billion renminbi (US$38 billion). Its total sales area reached 20 million square meters. And Vanke's business covered 55 Chinese cities, with its national market share at 3%. It is dominant in China's mega-clusters of the Pearl River Delta, the Yangtze River Delta and the Bohai Rim Economic Circle. Today, China Vanke is the world's largest real estate company, employing approximately 16,000 employees in 28 locations.

However, all of this success has now had an interesting development. As of this writing in 2016, Vanke is fighting against China's first major takeover battle. Financial speculators, Chinese red chips and other real estate players are all in the mix. Vanke's success, its listed status and the low shareholding of Wang Shi himself has put the company in play.

But the story of Vanke is one we will see again and again in this book: an entrepreneur was in the right place at the right time, caught one of the six mega-trends and then rocketed upwards at astonishing speeds.

Today, at 65, Shi remains Chairman of China Vanke and is one of China's most famous businessmen. He is also a philanthropist and a noted environmentalist. And he is a particularly well-known mountain-climbing enthusiast, having conquered the highest peaks of all seven continents.

Wang Shi – Chairman, mountain climber, philanthropist, environmentalist
(Photo: Imaginechina)

THE SECRET OF HIS SUCCESS

We have argued that China Vanke's meteoric rise followed from catching the urbanization mega-trend. That means being in the right place at the right time – which 1988 Shenzhen absolutely was. However, they were certainly not the only ones there doing real estate. So how did they become number one?

The secret to Vanke's success was cost-efficiency and speed. While many developers focused on building landmark real estate projects or on projects with out-sized financial returns (say, 100 percent), China Vanke focused on speed. Shi has said he focused on projects with 25% returns and would drop any project over 40%. This reflects a core concept of Vanke's operating strategy: expediting turnover while driving trading volume, even if it means passing on higher return projects.

Vanke has a business model it calls "5-9-8-6." Start construction within five months of land purchase. Kick-off sales in the ninth month. Achieve 80% of the target in the first month. And sell out 60% once the project has opened up for sales. This enables the company to retrieve cash faster than its competitors. It can then re-invest to acquire more land for construction and development.

We argue that their focus on speed, turnover and covering a large network of cities enabled them to ride the urbanization wave more effectively than others. They also chose to focus exclusively on real estate. Early-on, they sold 10 other promising businesses so they could focus entirely on residential real estate.

China Vanke's unique eco-friendly "horizontal skyscraper" headquarters in Shenzhen (Photo: Imaginechina)

***

That's most of our point for this chapter. We've given you a big trend. We've given you a story. And we've made a few key points. But there are some fascinating aspects to urbanization. And we have detailed six more of them below. These can be skimmed if you are trying to keep this book to one hour

KEY POINT #4: CHINA IS A SERIES OF CLUSTERS, NOT A CONTINENT

Looking at China today, what you don't see is an integrated continental economy. You don't see infrastructure connecting each part of the country, like say in the United States and Europe. That is likely the future but not yet the present.

If you look at the population and the existing infrastructure, what you actually see is a series of "clusters". You see clusters of cities with over 60 million people. For example, Beijing / Tianjin in the North is actually a cluster of 28 cities – all tightly interconnected by roads, rail and other infrastructure. Qingdao, well known for its beer, is actually part of a 35-city cluster.

China has more than 20 of these clusters (shown below), and each of these clusters is about the size of a European country. According to government plans, China's main clusters will cover 80 percent of GDP and 60 percent of the population.

Chinese city clusters with average populations of 60M

Beijing / Tianjin = 28 cities
Shanghai = 58 cities
Guangzhou / Shenzhen = 23 cities
Shenyang / Dalian = 22 cities
Qingdao / Jinan = 35 cities
Zhengzhou = 23 cities
Chengdu / Chongqing = 31 cities
Wuhan = 27 cities
Changsha = 20 cities
Xian = 8 cities
Xiamen / Fuzhou = 14 cities

Source: McKinsey & Company

If you think about China as a series of clusters, and not as a continent, a lot of things make more sense – especially urbanization and infrastructure. Much of the highly publicized high speed rail and other infrastructure projects are about creating clusters. It is about making it possible for people and goods to travel cheaply and quickly within a cluster.

And these clusters do vary by income, demographics and social structure. Shenzhen, the original migrant megacity, is markedly younger than Guangzhou, its cousin 2 hours away. Shanghai has more rich people than nearly all of the inland clusters combined. And in Beijing, household sizes are shrinking faster than in any other cluster. It is an interesting phenomenon to keep track of.

Much of the new infrastructure, such as high-speed rail, is about building clusters (Photo: redstone / iStockphoto)

KEY POINT #5: URBANIZATION = BIG PROBLEMS = BIG OPPORTUNITIES

As mentioned, urbanization is creating a need for housing and infrastructure that is ongoing. But infrastructure is only part of the problem. These new urban populations are creating increasing pressure on government for security (e.g., police), for public services (e.g., sanitation, buses, etc.), for government funding, and for natural resources, particularly water and energy.

Imagine being a government city official facing such an inflow of people every year. How many roads will you build this year? How many new subway lines? How will you deal with rising pollution levels and crime? How will you grow the GDP? How do you plan for rapid growth across virtually every aspect of urban life? It's a daunting job.

There is some fascinating work by McKinsey on strategies for city development (we are obviously biased here). One interesting project is the Urban China Initiative, which is a joint project between McKinsey, Tsinghua University's School of Public Policy and Management and Columbia University. Central to this project is the question of how do you balance economic development, resource needs, environmental impact and social well-being. You can find the research at www.urbanchinainitiative.org.

WATER IS THE BIGGEST PROBLEM

A good example of how urbanization creates both big problems and big opportunities is the water situation.

China is one of the world's thirstiest countries. There is limited water supply in general and agriculture uses the majority of fresh water today (about 62 percent). And as China grows wealthier, this agricultural usage is increasing (wealthier countries eat more). And what's more, industrial and municipal uses are actually growing faster than agricultural uses. So across the board, we are seeing increasing demand for a fairly small water supply.

Exacerbating this supply problem is the deteriorating water quality in China. By most estimates, 60 percent of underground water and 40 percent of rivers are seriously polluted and unfit for use. This is largely due to the 75 billion tons of sewage and wastewater that has been discharged into them. One extreme example of this river dumping phenomenon was the surprising appearance of 2,800 dead pigs in Shanghai's main river in the summer of 2013. The pigs had been dumped upstream into the river and floated into downtown Shanghai one Monday morning.

Overall, approximately 300 million rural dwellers have no access to safe drinking water. And when you combine this water situation with the urbanization mega-trend, it is not surprising that two-thirds of Chinese cities today are short of water.

Chinese rivers can change color based on what has recently been dumped into them (Photo: Zhang Xiaoli / ChinaFotoPress)

The government's response to this problem thus far has been to increase the water supply. In particular, they have been building large projects such as the South-North Water Transfer Project. This is a multi-decade, multi-billion dollar infrastructure project that creates Western, Central and Eastern water routes. All three routes aim to divert water from the Yangtze River to the Yellow River and Hai River. The project was originally expected to cost $62 billion – more than twice as much as the Three Gorges Dam - but over $80 billion had been spent by 2014. But supply alone cannot solve the problem. Next on the agenda is water conservation and treatment. And the government is openly supporting innovation in this area.

The Three Gorges Dam (Photo: Thomas Barrat / Shutterstock)

All this creates big business opportunities. According to Chen Lei, Minister of Water Resources, China plans to invest $636 billion on water-related projects through 2020. These projects will be geared toward treating heavily polluted rivers and lakes and toward improving water ecosystems in ecologically fragile areas. For example, China currently accounts for about 90 percent of the annual global investment in forests, wetlands and other ecosystems that help keep human water supplies clean.

KEY POINT #6: IT'S MOSTLY ABOUT THE CONSTRUCTION

Urbanization, real estate and infrastructure all get mixed together as topics. The numbers can get confusing. When this happens, just check the construction spending. It's mostly about the construction. Real estate accounts for about 20-22 percent of the total national investment in fixed assets. And construction employs over 100 million people directly or indirectly.

Construction also ties to other industries. Real estate is a factor in the sale of consumer appliances, furnishings, and anything else that can be put in an apartment, house, office or warehouse. And obviously, construction and real estate play a decisive role in the building material industries. Each year in China, 25 percent of steel, 70 percent of cement, 40 percent of wood, 70 percent of plate glass and 25 percent of plastics are used in real estate development and construction.

Economically, it's still mostly about construction
(© Zhang Yongxin/123RF Stock Photo)

Basically, it's all about construction. It doesn't mean it is sustainable or even necessarily a good idea. But it is where the biggest dollars from urbanization are located.

FINAL POINT: URBANIZATION IS A SOCIAL PHENOMENON

Cities have all aspects of human life: family, culture, health, politics, work, art, environment, and just about everything else. So urbanization affects almost everything. And it is putting the majority of the Chinese population into close contact with each other for the first time. Such close contact will change everyone. Ultimately, Chinese urbanization is the largest social experiment ever seen.

The long-term implications of this on Chinese social, cultural and lifestyle norms are anyone's guess. Alongside the many positive outcomes of urbanization (such as increasing incomes) are some that may challenge the fabric of Chinese society. There is without question a widening income gap between rural and urban populations– and between urban professionals and migrant workers (the unofficial urban lower class). Pollution has very quickly become a major priority for urban residents. And urban life is very different than the slow-moving, family-centric village lifestyle that dominated China for centuries. And all these changes are happening very quickly.

So it is worth keeping in mind that when people talk about 1 billion Chinese city dwellers, nobody really knows what that means.

Is it all too much too fast? A 13-story building falls over in Shanghai in 2009
(Photo: Imaginechina)

MEGA-TREND #2: HUGE MANUFACTURING SCALE

Our second mega-trend is Chinese manufacturing scale. And this is likely the most well-known trend to Western observers. Consumers around the world are long accustomed to things being "Made in China." Shoes, bicycles, toys, tables, and so on. China is the "world's workshop". It is also sometimes known as "the place where underwear comes from."

Chinese manufactured products outbound to the world at Qingdao port
(Photo: Imaginechina)

But this trend is not just about manufacturing. It's about manufacturing scale. It's about being a lot bigger than your competitors in the market.

This is what investors call economies of scale. It is the situation where you are so much larger than your competitors, relative to the market, that you can outspend them on research, factories, fixed assets, marketing and other fixed costs. It's the point where you are very difficult to compete with due to your scale. It's what Warren Buffett calls the "survival of the fattest." What we see in China today is exceptionally large manufacturing scale that is creating an entrenched position over time.

A few facts about China's manufacturing juggernaut:

- China is the world's largest manufacturer with over $2.9 trillion in manufacturing value-add. Its manufacturing base has increased by over 20 times in the last 30 years.

- China produces 80 percent of the world's air-conditioners, 90 percent of the world's personal computers, 75 percent of the world's solar panels, 70 percent of the world's cell phones, and 63 percent of the world's shoes.

- Manufacturing is 40 percent of the Chinese GDP and directly employs 130 million people, a number that has been relatively stable over the past decades.

- Within this space, there are a huge number of Chinese companies fiercely competing. For example, there are now over 30,000 building materials companies in China making everything from ceramic tiles to wood flooring.

Chinese exports over time (Billions USD)

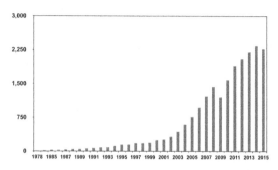

Source: China Statistical Yearbook, CEIC

China has several big advantages in manufacturing. One is low labor costs. Salaries have on average been 15 percent of the US at $2.1 per hour versus $35 (although this is changing fast). Another advantage is a rapidly growing domestic market. For example, annual domestic car sales in China exceed 20 million cars, greater than the US at around 16 million. Other advantages are infrastructure investments, engineering talent and a rapidly developing supplier base. But economies of scale is really the big advantage for Chinese manufacturers.

This does not mean Chinese manufacturers do not have problems. They are dealing with a host of difficult issues: rising labor costs, a complicated global supply chain, demanding domestic and global customers, volatility from a global market, and so on. Being #1 isn't easy.

And it is worth noting two major manufacturer strategies happening today:

- There is a movement from low-tech assembly to more high tech manufacturing. Go back ten years and the majority of Chinese exports were basic items like toys and textiles. Today, the majority of China's exports are classified as technology. This includes phones, engine systems, and cars. The direct value-add of China's exports has increased from 20% in the 1980s to 50% today.

- The second strategy is a shift geographically from the more expensive coastal areas into cheaper Central and Western China. Improving infrastructure, growing local markets, cheaper labor and a robust educational endowment are enabling local governments in these regions to compete for the business of cost-sensitive companies. In Chengdu, the home of China's giant pandas, a high-tech cluster is growing around Intel, AMD, HP, and other global hi-tech players. In Wuhan, the Donghu Optical Fiber Zone takes advantage of Wuhan's supply of science graduates. These are situations that are worth watching.

Twenty years ago, Chinese manufacturing was mostly clothes and simple products
(© Xiaodong Sun/123RF Stock Photo)

Today, Chinese manufacturing is mostly technology
(© Dmitry Kalinovsky/123RF Stock Photo)

Coming back to our main chart, huge manufacturing scale is the second mega-trend.

The 6 China Megatrends

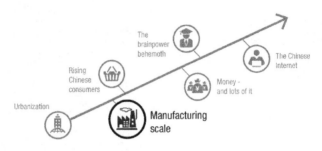

THE STORY OF REN ZHENGFEI AND HUAWEI

Let's switch again from numbers to a (hopefully) cool story. A good example of a company that rode the manufacturing mega-trend to great heights is Huawei Technologies. It is arguably the most global Chinese company today.

Founded by Ren Zhengfei in 1987, Huawei has grown to become the world's largest telecommunications equipment company. They make mobile network routers, phone interchanges, handhelds, Wi-Fi devices, and just about every other manufactured product associated with telecommunications. They operate in 170 countries and generate revenue of $60 billion (2015). The company has 170,000 employees and operates R&D institutes in China, the United States, Germany, Sweden, Ireland, India, Russia, and Turkey. In 2012, they achieved their long-stated goal of dethroning Ericsson as the world's largest telecommunications network equipment company. Although who is #1 and #2 does sort of depend on what definition you use.

Another Shenzhen Rags to Riches Story

Founder Ren Zhengfei was born in 1944 in Guizhou in southwestern China. In many ways, the story of Ren Zhengfei parallels that of Wang Shi in the previous chapter. They both were born in the same time period in Southwestern China. They both struggled in the 1970s, in the years prior to the opening of China. And they both eventually made their fortunes by being in Shenzhen at the right time.

Zhengfei was born the son of two teachers, both of whom worked at the No.1 Middle School of Duyun. And while Wang Shi's family had a somewhat helpful history with the People's Liberation Army (PLA), Zhengfei's family had a history with the Kuomintang (the Chinese Nationalist Party). His father had worked as an accounts clerk for a Kuomintang arms factory in Guangzhou.

After high school, Zhengfei moved north and attended Chongqing University of Civil Engineering and Architecture. He then joined the Research Institute of the PLA as a military technologist. It was at this point that he began to distinguish himself with his technical ability. If Shi is at heart a deal maker, Zhengfei is a technologist. He is reported to have contributed many technical innovations as a PLA officer and was selected as a delegate to attend the National Science Conference in 1978.

Fast-forward to the early 1980s and Zhengfei, at the age of 38, had just retired from the PLA during a "downsizing" of 50,000 officers. China was beginning its historic opening and Zhengfei began working in the electronics industry. Again, similar to Wang Shi, there was almost no indication of the heights to which he would soon rise.

The decisive move came in 1987, when at the age of 43, Zhengfei decided to start a new life in Shenzhen. He arrived in booming Shenzhen and founded a tiny electronics company, named Huawei. The initial registered capital was about $5,000.

Again, similar to China Vanke, Huawei initially acted as an agent for products being brought into China. Their first contract was as a sales agency for a private branch exchange (PBX) made by a Hong Kong company. PBXs are basically internal phone switching stations. It lets a company connect many internal phones lines with just a few external phone lines (i.e., not every phone in the company calls outside on its own line).

But while Shi used his agent and trading contracts to fund his initial real estate deals, Zhengfei used them to learn more about technology. His goal was to establish his own technology company and foreign companies had far greater expertise. So Zhengfei and his coworkers reinvested most of their earnings back into the company and focused on the development of their own telecommunications products. By 1993, Huawei had developed its own PBX product for the Chinese market.

Fortunately for Huawei, both manufacturing and the telecommunication equipment market were surging. Huawei expanded its product line and became adept at targeting small niche markets. Competing with multinationals like Ericsson in Beijing and Shanghai would have been impossible. So they focused on rural and third tier cities, where the demand was less but so was the competition. Targeting second and third tier cities is a common strategy for Chinese manufacturers and will be discussed more later. It is a basically a strategy for avoiding foreign competitors who have superior technology but tend to focus on easier to reach first tier cities.

Huawei grew rapidly and by 1995 was earning annual revenue of $163 million, mostly from selling its telecommunication equipment to small enterprises and hotels in the rural areas of China.

In 1997, Huawei made another decisive move. They turned to international expansion. This both opened up new potential markets and avoided difficulties in the domestic China market. They did their first international contract (fixed line network products) with Hutchison Whampoa in Hong Kong. And from there, they expanded globally like no Chinese company had before. They went across Asia. They went to the Middle East. They went to Africa. In many ways, Huawei's strategy for global expansion resembled their domestic market strategy. They targeted less-developed areas, where sales were lower but so was competition. Many of Huawei's early sales came from Southeast Asia, Africa, and Eastern Europe, all areas somewhat neglected by major global players.

Their primary strategy was to use Chinese manufacturing scale to offer products at low prices. In some cases, Huawei even offered the initial system for free for an extended period of time and they only received money once the user count reached a certain number.

How Chinese manufacturers use their economic scale to defeat multinationals is an important topic. Yes, they have a low cost advantage and this can be devastating. But they also have an ability to customize products as they use labor instead of automated factories. Such customization is difficult for multinationals to match, as it requires doing costly reconfigurations to their automated factories. So Chinese manufacturers will often use a "low cost + customization" strategy against multinationals. This is particularly effective when the target is a smaller niche market, such as the Middle East or a 3rd tier Chinese city. Multinationals facing this situation will often decide it isn't worth it.

Huawei started to gain global market share in the late 1990s and by 2002, international sales had reached $552 million. In 2005, international contract orders exceeded domestic sales for the first time. By 2009, Huawei was the number two player in the global telecommunications equipment market, behind only Ericsson. By the time Huawei became number one in 2012, it was earning over two-thirds of its $36 billion in revenue outside of China. Huawei's spectacular rise is a story about deploying Chinese manufacturing scale (our mega-trend) in global markets.

Also during these years, Huawei expanded out of pure equipment manufacturing into services and devices, such as smart phones and tablets. It is currently a top 3 smart phone vendor, behind only Apple and Samsung. Huawei ads now cover Rotterdam trams, Berlin buildings and the jerseys of Arsenal and AC Milan.

Today, Huawei is one of China's most famous brands. And it is regarded as one of the leading hi-tech companies in the world, along with Apple, Samsung, and Sony. Time Magazine lists Zhengfei as one of its 100 most influential people. And in 2010, Fast Company named Huawei as the fifth most innovative company in the world.

Zhengfei remains President of Huawei. He is one of China's most famous billionaires but is also one of its most media shy. In 2013, approaching the age of 70, he gave his first media interview ever while on a trip to New Zealand.

Ren Zhengfei, Founder and President of Huawei (Photo: Imaginechina)

THE SECRET OF HUAWEI'S SUCCESS

As in the case of China Vanke, Huawei was in the right place at the right time. While Vanke rode the urbanization mega-trend, Huawei rode the Chinese manufacturing mega-trend. And this enabled them to win not just in China, but also globally. However, the key question again is how did they win? What set them apart from their many Chinese competitors? And later against companies like Ericsson, Cisco and Motorola?

Huawei's global success appears to be the result of a very smart application of China's manufacturing advantages against specific international markets. Zhengfei also implemented certain guidelines that defined Huawei for much of its twenty-year history - including:

1. Focus only on the telecommunication industry
2. Spend 10% of yearly income on R&D
3. Invest heavily in human capital
4. Cultivate the "wolf spirit"

It is worth commenting on these briefly.

First they have a strict telecommunications focus. There were tremendous opportunities for Huawei to diversify its business along the way. They were a large and profitable company in Shenzhen during the boom years. Why not go into real estate? Why not go into other manufacturing sectors? Many large Chinese companies became multi-business conglomerates during this period. But Zhengfei chose to focus only on the telecommunication industry – even if it meant leaving the Chinese market and going to Africa and Latin America. This decision paid off, as Huawei focused its financial resources and manufacturing scale on winning market after market.

The guideline for human capital is interesting. High employee turnover is a big problem in China, especially for engineers. Huawei developed a unique compensation structure to address this. It is reported that Zhengfei owns only 1.48 percent of the company's shares. The other 98 percent are 'Virtual Restricted Shares', which are reportedly owned by employee shareholders. We are qualifying these statements because it is not totally clear. Huawei's employees apparently win the right to purchase shares at a good price in proportion to their time at the company. So their shares increase with the time spent at Huawei. As a result, Huawei has been able to maintain a team of high-quality engineers over the long-term.

Finally, Zhengfei defined what he calls a "wolf spirit" for the company. He described this as three key factors: extreme resilience in the face of failure, a strong tolerance for self-sacrifice, and a sharp predator instinct. He has said that in order for Huawei to become a global player, each member of Huawei must have such spirit. Huawei may not be a lion like Ericsson, but they can challenge it like a pack of wolves that will exhaust the lion.

Wolves are also apparently not easily frightened. During Libya's civil war in 2012, Huawei was the only international company that did not pull its employees from the country.

***

Per our approach, we have given you a trend and a short story. That's most of this chapter. We have also detailed four additional key points below. If these get tedious, just read the headlines and jump to the next chapter.

KEY POINT #1: LOW COST IS HOW YOU WIN IN MOST OF CHINA

China is a "must win" market for many multinational companies (MNCs). And when they first entered China in the 1990s, local Chinese manufacturers were largely a negligible threat. Siemens and Johnson & Johnson simply did not worry about Chinese manufacturers suddenly switching from making bicycles to making ultrasound machines. Most MNCs entered China with powerful brands, advanced technologies, and lots of cash. Their main competitive threats were other MNCs, the same old foes they were used to fighting in other markets.

Much of Chinese manufacturing has historically been low-cost (usually polluting) factories (Photo: Prill Mediendesign & Fotografie / iStockphoto)

Fast forward to 2016 and competition in China is fierce, especially between Chinese and multinational manufacturers. Now everyone has cash. Now everyone has scale. And while MNCs still have some brand and technology advantages, Chinese manufacturers have cost and other advantages. As Warren Buffett's partner Charlie Munger has said, "At Berkshire Hathaway, we do not like to compete against Chinese manufacturers."

A good example of how this domestic versus foreigner competition is playing out is in the medical device market, including the ultrasound machines just mentioned.

Chinese healthcare spending will more than double in the next 8 years. You combine that with the fact there are 1.3 billion Chinese and it is no surprise that most all the ultrasound and other major medical device manufacturers are fighting for China. GE Healthcare, Philips, Abbott Laboratory, Johnson & Johnson, and Medtronic all have a local presence. And today, these MNCs control much of the first tier markets for high end products like MRIs and ultrasounds. If you go to a hospital in Beijing or Guangzhou, you will likely find foreign MRI machines.

However, this medium-to-high end market is only about 25 percent of the total Chinese market for medical devices. Once you move out of the top-tier cities, hospitals become filled with products from Chinese companies such as Mindray, KangHui, Weigo, and MicroPort. Today, more than 50 percent of the medical device market is owned by Chinese manufacturers. We are now a world away from Chinese manufacturers making bicycles and shoes.

How did this happen? How did Chinese manufacturers capture a dominant share of the market in a hi-tech sector?

It's mostly about low cost - and Chinese manufacturers have big advantages here. For example, Western coronary stents, which are often priced around $3,200, can be found offered by Chinese companies at $2,500 and below.

Additionally, Chinese companies are much better at selling to hospitals in harder-to-reach rural markets. This is similar to Huawei's early strategy: focus on smaller, harder-to-reach markets and offer low prices. Generally, the large multinationals will give up. And you can pick off the customers one by one. Like wolves circling their prey, Chinese manufacturers are picking off MNC customers one by one.

It gets worse. Despite selling at low prices, Chinese players are enjoying high margins. Orthopedics companies such as KangHui and Weigo are estimated to have profit margins of 40 to 50 percent. MicroPort and Lepu are estimated to have margins of 35 percent to 55 percent. These low cost competitors are generating lots of cash. And they are reinvesting it into building scale and developing technology. Their products are getting better and better.

However, multinationals are also manufacturing in China. So don't they have the same cost structure? How are domestic companies still cheaper?

It turns out being a low-cost medical device manufacturer in China requires lower product costs, broader and cheaper distribution, and good relationships with State-owned hospitals.

In fact, much of the cost advantage that Chinese producers possess comes from selling and distribution. China is a vast country, with over 15,000 hospital distributors. The lack of nationwide distributors makes it particularly difficult to penetrate low-tier cities and rural areas. Chinese companies are particularly good at selling and distributing widely and cheaply in China. For example, Chinese Mindray manages more than 1,500 sales personnel and has the largest distribution network in China.

So the fight for the domestic China market is mostly about low cost. But it's a bit more complicated than it first appears.

KEY POINT #2: THE KEY FIGHT IS THE MIDDLE MARKET

As discussed, Chinese medical device makers use lower cost to dominate in the lower markets. MNCs tend to do well in the top-tier markets and rely more on brand and technology.

Here's the problem. Chinese manufacturers keep investing into expanding sales, production capacity, and R&D. For example in 2011, Chinese Mindray invests 10 percent of its revenue in R&D and launches 10 new products annually. They are all trying to become high-end medical device manufacturers. And they are moving up into the middle and higher segments where the MNCs live.

This leads to the **fight in the middle**. Chinese companies are rapidly upgrading their technology and moving up into the second and first tier cities. Foreign companies are trying to drop their costs and move down to second and third tier cities. You frequently see MNCs acquiring Chinese companies to do this.

You see this fight in the middle in sector after sector. It's a big part of the evolution of the China market for manufactured products. Sometimes the Chinese company wins and sometimes the MNC wins. But the fight in the middle is the one to watch.

KEY POINT #3: CHINESE MANUFACTURERS ARE GOING GLOBAL, SORT OF

The fight in the middle is a dynamic of domestic manufacturing. What about international markets? What about in the US?

Going global is a popular mantra for Chinese CEOs today. More than a decade ago, China had 11 companies on the Fortune Global 500 list. In 2014, the number is 95. This makes China the #2 country in terms of Fortune Global 500 companies (after the US).

But a closer look shows it is not so straightforward. Most Chinese companies on the Fortune Global list are there due to their scale in the Chinese market, not because they have gone global. And the ability of Chinese manufacturers to compete directly in Western markets is unclear.

Most of the Chinese globalization activity we see today is not about capturing Western markets. In developing economies, it is about seeking smaller unsaturated markets and natural resources. In advanced economies, it is usually about acquiring technology, brands and managerial know-how. And then using this in China.

But the ultimate goal is to become a true Chinese multinational. And that means winning in Western markets directly. Against this goal, most Chinese aspirants are establishing foreign R&D centers, creating joint ventures, and pursuing organic growth in high-end markets. They are preparing to compete directly against powerful Western incumbents.

FINAL POINT: THE FIGHT FOR MANUFACTURING SCALE IS OFTEN ABOUT BEING THE LAST MAN STANDING

Chinese companies frequently win in China by building manufacturing economies of scale. And this fight for scale frequently resembles a game of chicken. You have to have the willingness to add large amounts of capacity. You keep building more factories than your competitor. And then the biggest competitor makes a little money, second place breaks even and everyone else swims in red ink. Ultimately, the most efficient player is the only one left standing when the market finally catches up to these aggressive capacity builds.

The Western press is often populated with commentary about how China is inefficient. About how there is too much capacity, say in blast furnaces. And that this is a reflection of China's politico-economic system. More often than not, this is just "last man standing" playing itself out. Everyone builds capacity and then everyone but a few players die.

Chinese companies will often repeat this last man standing strategy in other emerging markets. They build big, sell cheap and try to be the only company to survive the losses this entails. And it often works.

But as mentioned, this strategy has proven difficult in Western markets - especially against companies with both established market share and brand equity. Brand equity is the West's primary firewall against Chinese manufacturing scale.

From Chinese manufacturers to the world (photo: tcly / Shutterstock)

MEGA-TREND #3: RISING CHINESE CONSUMERS

Rising Chinese consumer power is our third mega-trend. The previously discussed trends have been serious economic forces for two decades. This one has only started really moving in the last 10 years, as shown in the exhibit below.

Chinese mobile subscribers, Internet users and consumer expenditures over time

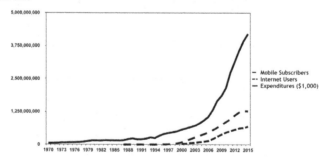

Source: World Bank, OECD, World Development Indicators Database, CEIC

While consumers buying goods and services is fairly simple on the surface, it is actually greatly impacted by psychology, culture, and individual behavior. So this is a far more unpredictable mega-trend than the previous two. We are going to make six key points and then tell you the stories of a couple of different companies that captured this trend.

The 6 China Megatrends

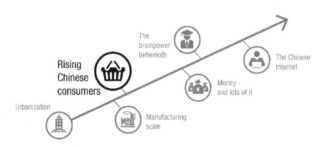

KEY POINT #1: CHINESE (AND ASIAN) MIDDLE CLASS CONSUMERS ARE THE FUTURE

China tends to get grouped in with other developing countries – typically Brazil, Russia and India. It really makes no sense (what exactly does Chongqing have to do with Cancun?). But 20 years ago, to portfolio managers sitting in New York, all these places seemed both far away and kind of strange. So they were grouped. And even today, you read a lot about the BRICs and emerging market consumers. This is a mistake.

Because when you look at actual incomes, it is clear that the future of the global economy is China and Asia. Middle class incomes in Asia will dwarf everything else. Forget Latin America (no offense). Forget Africa (same). It is the middle class of Asia that is the biggest economic growth engine going forward – similar to how the American middle class was the growth engine of the past century.

The numbers show this pretty clearly. Over the past 30 years, approximately 300 million people have moved into China's middle class. And according to the OECD Development Centre, the forecast is for another 200 million people to move into the middle class by 2026. This means the Asia Pacific region, which in 2009 represented 18% of the world's middle class, will reach 66 percent by 2030. Let's repeat that. Over the next 15 years, Asia will go from 20 percent to 66 percent of the world's middle class.

At the same time, the developed markets of North America and Europe, which held a combined 54 percent of the global middle class in 2009, are forecast to drop to only 21 percent by 2030. Basically, follow the money. Asia's middle class consumers are the future. Learn Mandarin.

KEY POINT #2: CHINESE CONSUMERS ARE STILL MOSTLY FOCUSED ON "VALUE FOR MONEY"

China has followed the path of a typical developing country. It began as an export-oriented economy with low labor costs. And prior to joining the World Trade Organization in 2001, it had a protectionist strategy marked by high import barriers. This gave Chinese companies time to get their footing without being overwhelmed by foreign multinationals. Those barriers have since come down somewhat.

A fairly typical shopping day in Shanghai
(© whitetag/123RF Stock Photo)

The Chinese consumer-focused companies that have done well over the past fifteen years are now giants. They are cash rich. And their strategy has mostly been to offer "value for money" products. They offer basic furniture, inexpensive but reliable washing machines, small standardized residential apartments, and so on. They have focused on delivering life's basics at a cheap price and at an acceptable quality level. Think all the stuff you find in a Wal-Mart, a lot of which is from China. The biggest factor is getting "value for money."

That brings us to our first story. A story about how you can build a huge empire by providing even the simplest of products to this massive consumer population.

THE STORY OF MASTER KONG'S NOODLE EMPIRE

Warren Buffett has a great comment about why he invested in American razor-maker Gillette. He said he found it comforting to know that every night while he slept "beards are growing all over the world."

If there is an equivalent to this in China, it is instant noodle maker Master Kong (Kang-Shi-Fu in Mandarin). China has 1.3 billion consumers and, while sleeping at night, you can rest assured that they are all getting hungry. And many are eventually going to go for a bowl of noodles. It's not a universal law like gravity but it's pretty close.

Enter Master Kong, which was launched in Tianjin in 1992 by the Wei brothers out of Taiwan. Their product was a simple and cheap bowl of instant noodles with a cartoon of a chubby chef as their logo. As a consumer products story, this is really as simple as you can get. You produce and distribute instant noodle packages. Consumers add hot water and eat. There is really not much more to tell. The interesting question here is "how successful can a simple instant noodle company possibly become?"

The parent company Tingyi Holding Company had over 69,000 employees and $9 billion in revenue in 2015. In 2015, Master Kong was also the most chosen brand of

Chinese consumers according to research firm Kantar. Its products are bought an average of 8.8 times a year by 90% of the urban Chinese households. In China, instant noodles (and other consumer products) are big business. And they have made the Wei brothers billionaires.

Tingyi is also active in other consumer-focused ventures. In 1996, they began expanding into the beverage business and by 2007 they were number one in the Chinese soft drink market. Their bottled tea products are particularly popular. In 2011, Tingyi signed a strategic alliance with PepsiCo to be the exclusive manufacturer, bottler and distributor of Pepsi's non-alcoholic drinks in China.

For Chinese consumers, these products were not a big step up. People had been buying noodles and tea in stores and restaurants for hundreds of years. What Master Kong offered was offer a standardized, quality product at a low price. Many of the Chinese consumer success stories thus far are like this.

In 2015, Chinese GDP per capita was approximately $6,500. So the average Chinese consumer still doesn't have a lot of excess money - and is culturally price sensitive anyway. Most of the Chinese consumer giant companies we will mention succeeded because they kept it simple, focused on "value for money", and then got big as fast as they could.

KEY POINT #3: THE NEXT BIG THING IS MORE EMOTIONAL CONSUMERS

A good way to think about the past 30 years in China is as one big consumer transition. People went from "subsistence living" to being able to purchase the full range of life's basic goods. They went from focusing on food and shelter to filling up their homes with basic products like washing machines and sneakers. This consumer transition tracked growth in GDP per capita from $200 in 1982 to aproximately $5,500 in 2015. And it was the "value for money" consumer companies that really capitalized on this.

We are now seeing another big transition. China's consumers are starting to look to more emotional and aspirational needs. They are increasingly going to Starbucks, traveling overseas, wearing luxury brands, buying iPhones, going to the movies and choosing furniture based on how it fits their sense of self. Suddenly it's not all about having the basics at a good price. Urban and affluent consumers, in particular, are attaching greater importance to the emotional benefits they receive from purchases.

The interesting thing is these more emotional Chinese consumers are starting to shop similar to Westerners (and South Koreans). And not just a little bit. Their purchasing habits are shifting to an almost identical pattern to what you see in places like London and Chicago. This also has an interesting tie to urbanization. As consumers move from the countryside into the city, their spending patterns change more quickly and they become more similar Westerners in consumption.

THE STORY OF THE BROTHERS WANG AND THE BROTHERS WARNER

Meeting emotional needs does not mean just offering luxury or branded products. For example, the entertainment industry is an almost entirely emotional offering.

A good story for this is that of the Huayi Brothers, China's largest movie and television studio. It's a fascinating story but it is not the stunning "rags to riches" story we have seen in other cases. In 2010, after sixteen years of operations, Huayi Brothers' revenue and earnings were still only $168M and $10M respectively. So this is a story about rising consumer power but there are some interesting differences to the explosive growth seen in Master Kong's noodle empire.

Huayi Brothers was founded in 1994 by Wang Zhongjun and Wang Zhonglei (i.e., the Wang brothers). Their initial idea was to focus on advertising services. They have since admitted that their business plan was pretty vague at that point. They basically just jumped in and opened an office big enough to impress potential clients. Zhongjun would later describe this early period as unfocused and high pressure (they had hired about 30 staff and had only enough cash for about six months).

After multiple attempts at various advertising projects, they eventually settled on doing high quality signage for local banks. Banks need higher quality signs than most other stores. And they have lots of branches and therefore need lots of signs. The brothers eventually made several million dollars by producing such signs. It was these early advertising projects that got them enough capital to start making films.

In 1998, they made their jump into film production. And they adopted a model similar to the early days of Hollywood. They built relationships with top actors and directors. It bore a close resemblance to the early days of Warner Brothers. In fact, the Wang brothers would soon be referred to as the "Warner Brothers of China".

They added a talent agency. They added television production and music. Over ten years, they did a gradual expansion into most aspects of entertainment. But the secret to their success was arguably their relationships with a few key directors and stars. Feng Xiaogang, famous for a unique Chinese style of comedy, would become their most successful director.

Huayi Brothers Founders Wang Zhongjun and Wang Zhonglei
(Photo: Imaginechina)

Eventually, slowly, they became entertainment moguls, the Warner Brothers of China. But if instant noodles was a business that could quickly tap into growing Chinese consumer power, media was one of the slowest. Government controls were still tight and there were few movie theatres in China. The mega-trend was there but you couldn't really ride it financially. While "value for money" plays were exploding, the movie business was very slow in its growth financially.

Today, 22 years after its founding, Huayi Brothers is finally riding the consumer mega-trend. The Chinese cinema market has tripled in the past 3-4 years, reaching $7 billion in box office revenue today. In 2015 alone, over 8,000 cinema screens were added domestically, approximately 22 per day. China is now set to surpass the USA in movie productions, cinema screens and box office revenue.

And Huayi Brothers has finally started to experience the kind of growth seen by other consumer companies. From 2012 to 2016, their revenue jumped from $223 million to $615 million. They have also announced a plan to develop one of East Asia's largest TV and film studios, a $152 million project that will occupy 1,000 acres. They are now one of China's leading movie companies - and they are sitting at the intersection of rapidly rising and increasingly emotional Chinese consumers and gradually loosening government media controls.

KEY POINT #4: RISING CHINESE CONSUMER WEALTH HAS WEIRD EFFECTS

It is worth taking a step back and looking at how strange all of this is. Rising consumer wealth on such a huge scale creates some very strange phenomena.

For example, rising Chinese consumers are becoming meat-eaters. As societies become wealthier, people generally eat more meat. And we are seeing this play out in China in a startling way. For example, China is now the number one global consumer of pork and the number two consumer of chicken. China keeps a herd of 450 million pigs, about half of the global pig population. That factoid is kind of weird to try to visualize.

Some more on this:

- China consumes around 28% of the world's meat - including half the world's pork - according to the

OECD and FAO. Pork is the number one consumed meat product in China. Poultry is number two.

- China's pork market, at $202 billion, is two times larger than the total gross sales of smartphones in the country. China actually keeps a strategic reserve of frozen pork and living pigs. The government built the reserve following the outbreak of porcine blue-ear disease in 2006.

- In 2015, Chinese chicken consumption exceeded 12 million tons. This is almost equal to that of the US. However, average individual chicken consumption in the US is still more than four times higher.

- KFC is the number one fast food chain in China. KFC opened its first Chinese store in 1987 and now has over 4,000 restaurants. KFC has been averaging 1-2 new store openings per day over the past five years.

A good mental image for the "Chinese as meat eaters" phenomenon is provided by Tyson Foods. Tyson is one of the world's largest processors of pork, chicken, and beef. In 2009, they acquired the Shandong Xinchang Group, one of China's top five poultry producers. This created the Shandong Tyson Xinchang Foods Company - a company with facilities capable of processing over 3 million chickens per week. Annually their facilities can process over 156 million birds. That is a good mental image to consider. How big a factory do you need to kill 156 million chickens?

Anyway, our point is that it's easy to miss how strange all this really is. Next time someone cites "rising Chinese consumers" try to imagine how you actually kill 3 million chickens a week. The scale of this is very strange.

KEY POINT #5: FICKLE CHINESE CONSUMERS ARE DRIVING CHANGES AROUND THE WORLD

Being a royal pain is the defining characteristic of consumers. Consumers are perpetually demanding. On price, quality, service, convenience and just about every other dimension. They always want everything to be perfect. They always want more. And they always want it for less.

So what happens when a billion Chinese consumers start being really fickle and demanding?

Think about the previous "Chinese as meat-eaters" example. How much infrastructure and logistical support do you need to meet such a growing demand for meat? How many supermarkets? How many refrigerated trucks? What about just-in-time delivery? What about refrigeration and electricity in peoples' homes? And what happens to all of this when hundreds of millions of people now expect to have bananas in January, fresh fish daily and even more KFCs?

Demanding Chinese consumers are driving large changes in China and across the global economy. In infrastructure. In logistics. In supply. In farming. And consumer demands are ever increasing.

AS A RESULT, CHINA'S HOT NEW INDUSTRY IS FARMING

China's advancement over the past 30 years has brought modernization to most industries. But in some cases, systems remain undeveloped. Farming is one of those areas. Farming in much of China is still small scale and highly fragmented. Additionally, China as a country has no real advantages in farming. Per capita farmland is less than 40 percent of the global average and water resources are only a quarter. So even if farming were a developed sector (it's not), it would still face serious problems.

This has led to China's hot new investment sector: farming.

McKinsey has listed agri-business as one of the hottest areas for Chinese investment. The logic was pretty simple. There is rising demand from consumers and the entire supply chain needs to be improved: land, water, farming, fertilizer, technology, logistics, retail, etc. Almost everything.

Traditional small, inefficient farms still blanket much of the country
(© Sanphet Pruksaritanon/123RF Stock Photo)

This is leading to some interesting projects. Insects are being cultivated as a protein additive for animal feed. Scientists are breeding wasps that feed on the eggs of agriculture pests. And salmon and trout are even being farmed in the Gobi desert. Real estate company Shanghai Zhongfu and private equity player Legend Holdings, the parent of Lenovo, have both launched initiatives into large scale agricultural projects. Shanghai Zhongfu made an investment of more than $700 million to develop a sugar cane plantation in Western Australia. Even NetEase, of internet technology fame, has invested in a multi-million dollar pig growing operation in the province of Zhejiang.

Traditional Chinese farming
(© Dmitry Kalinovsky/123RF Stock Photo)

A final short story for this chapter.

THE STORY OF COFCO

Fortune 500 companies like Wal-Mart, Exxon-Mobil, Coca-Cola, and Google are symbolic in lots of ways. By their success and pure size, they symbolize their industries (e.g., Wal-Mart is synonymous with the US retail industry). They become representatives of their cities (e.g., Coca-Cola is a tourist destination in Atlanta). And they often become quasi-representatives of their home countries (e.g., GE's CEO travels on US trade missions).

So how about the China National Cereals, Oils and Foodstuffs Corporation (COFCO)? Not exactly a household name in the West.

Yet COFCO is arguably the single best symbol of Chinese consumers today. And yes, it is a Fortune 500 company and has been since 1994.

COFCO is today the largest supplier of products and services in the agriculture and food industries of China. Their mission is no less than to feed the world's largest population. And the scale of their operations is breath-taking. This is one of those situations where hyperbole is almost required.

A few examples to get your attention:

- COFCO products are purchased by over 90 percent of Chinese households.

- COFCO's three rice facilities can process a combined 2,250 tons of rice per day.

- COFCO has tea production capacity of 50,000 tons per year. Assuming the average teabag is 1.5 grams, that's enough to make 33 billion teabags per year.

- COFCO's Tunhe tomato operations can produce 500,000 metric tons of aseptic tomato paste per year - enough to fill over 1.3 billion 375g bottles.

Prior to the 1987 economic reforms which liberalized foreign trade and decollectivized agriculture, COFCO was the only importer and exporter of agricultural products in China. It was your classic central planning ministry which, in practice, meant setting agricultural imports and exports against annual plans for the country. The organization was effectively the food intermediary between China and the rest of the world.

And like most Chinese state enterprises, COFCO had had multiple organizational iterations, all with bureaucratic names. There was the China National Cereals, Oils and Foodstuffs Import and Export Corporation (CEROILS). There was the North China Grains Company. The Pig Bristles Company. And many others. We will spare you the chart with COFCO's bureaucratic permutations since 1949 (it's pretty impressive). But the primary purpose of each entity was to control agricultural imports and exports. It was the exclusive rights over these imports and exports that would later lead to COFCO's power as a commercial enterprise. Post-1987, COFCO evolved into a state-owned corporation. And like most Chinese state-owned enterprises (SOEs) it took on the operational workings of a commercial enterprise (mostly).

The interesting aspect is how dominant the company is today. This is a big difference from the other consumer companies we have mentioned.

Today, COFCO basically operates from the dinner table all the way back up to the fields. It straddles the whole agricultural and food processing value chain. COFCO employs nearly 100,000 people and is involved in virtually all areas of Chinese consumers' diets. It operates numerous companies, such as Mengniu Dairy, Tunhe (tomatoes), Fortune (edible oil), Great Wall Wine, Lohas (fruit juice), and Le Conte (chocolate). COFCO also has a partnership with Coca-Cola and is one of its bottlers and distributors in China (Coke entered China in 1980 through a partnership with COFCO).

From "field to the dining table" means directly operating in areas like milk factories in Inner Mongolia (© Zhang Yongxin /123RFStock Photo)

Unsurprisingly, with their success as China's food supplier, COFCO has also moved into other businesses. These include real estate, tourism, hotels, financial services, and insurance.

However, their strategy of "farm field to the dining tables" is really about overseeing the entire supply chain. They are aiming to manage the entire process by which agricultural products are converted into final consumer products. The main pillars of this are agriculture, processing, manufacturing, logistics and finance. Given the recent food scandals, this sort of control is becoming necessary to ensure quality. It's a good company to keep an eye on to understand Chinese agriculture and consumers.

There is an increasing focus on food safety-which in practice can be difficult to ensure.
(© Sakhorn Saengtongsamarnsin/123RF Stock Photo)

FINAL POINT: A CONSUMPTION ECONOMY?

In this chapter, and in this book, you have probably noticed that we have avoided many common macroeconomic and political topics. This is largely because Jeff is doing the editing and he despises both subjects (a joke, sort of).

But the first three mega-trends tee up an important question, frequently debated by economists. Will Chinese consumption provide a new growth model as investment and exports slow? And if so, will it be anytime soon?

The issue is GDP growth which has traditionally been 10% and has recently declined to 6 percent to 7 percent. Note:

these numbers are pretty fuzzy. China's GDP growth has historically come from investment and net exports. But both have been slowing and are externally dependent, creating some volatility. The question economists keep debating is whether domestic consumption (mega-trend #3) can provide a new growth engine for China's GDP.

It looks like the answer is yes (it will be a more important piece of GDP growth) and yes (it will make the difference between a medium and a slow growth China). Jonathan has just published a paper on this that goes into lots of detail (link here). And that is as far as we are going to comment on this.

We believe the winners from rising Chinese consumers are pretty obvious. Chinese consumers obviously benefit from an improving lifestyle. This is not a small thing. If you live in China, you always hear from Chinese friends about how they finally passed their driving test and are about to buy their first car. Or how they are sending their child to private school. Or how they are taking their first vacation overseas (typically to Thailand or France). This is all pretty inspiring.

And for business, anyone that can successfully tap into Chinese consumer habits has a good shot at ending up on the Fortune 1000 list. If you are big in the Chinese consumer market, you are big everywhere. Per our first point, Chinese middle class consumers are the future.

MEGA-TREND #4: MONEY – AND LOTS OF IT

Capitalism requires capital. And China's unique financial system is now moving huge amounts of capital around very quickly. Call it market socialism, state capitalism or what you will, but China's financial system today will impress any capitalist anywhere.

The macro numbers for China's banking and financial services sector are well-known and only mentioned here briefly. China has over $19 trillion in bank deposits and these grow by over $2 trillion every year. Foreign exchange reserves are very big ($3.2 trillion in 2016). China is the single largest foreign purchaser of US government debt. And the yearly trade surplus with the US has grown from zero in 1985 to over $365 billion in 2015. There is basically just a ton of cash.

The chart we like to show students is China's outbound foreign investment (below). This is what happened when China started to spend some of its cash pile overseas for the first time. We challenge you to find a curve like this in any other industry. You could have been the worst businessperson alive, but if you were in the right place when this started in 2004-5 (say in Australian natural resources), you would have made a lot of money.

China's outbound foreign direct investment (USD)

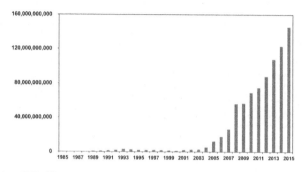

Source: MOFCOM, OECD, CEIC

However, the mega-trend here is not just the amount of money. It is the **volume, efficiency** and **sophistication** with which it now moves within China. We are interested in the financial architecture itself. And how money moves between projects, companies and financial institutions. Also, in light of recent credit concerns, the system's stability is a sigificant question.

The growth of the financial system is best symbolized by the picture below. It is Shanghai's financial district, Lujiazui, in 2013. Twenty years ago, this area was fields and small houses. The development of Liujiazui has been amazing. And it's not just money and buildings. It's the expertise, people, and systems. It's the whole financial eco-system you can see in this picture.

Shanghai's financial district - which was mostly fields and small houses in 1990

There have been two particularly important moments in the development of China's financial system.

The first was in 1979 when Shenzhen was designated a special territory for foreign economic activity and trade (later named a "Special Economic Zone"). For the financial system, this was the opening of China to both international capital and foreign financial expertise. It was no accident that this all started in Shenzhen, which is just across the border from international financial center Hong Kong. The movement of bankers, accountants, credit officers and lawyers across the border was a big part of the financial system's development.

The second event was on April 18, 1990 when Li Peng, then the Premier of China, announced a plan for the development of the Pudong region of Shanghai. This is the eastern part of Shanghai that lies between the Huang-pu River and the East China Sea. It contains the Lujiazui financial district shown in the previous picture. The plan effectively designated Shanghai as the financial capital of China (although Beijing is arguably as or more import-ant). The area along the Huangpu River was to focus on finance, commerce, exhibition and services, basically to become China's Wall Street. The area closer to the East China Sea was designated for shipping, trade, logistics and a few other things (including, eventually, a Disney-land).

But China's financial development is not just about two cities. It has been a nationwide training of hundreds of thousands of retail bankers, investment bankers, under-writers, loan officers, accountants, lawyers, traders, ana-lysts and other creatures of modern finance (or as Jeff calls them, "my people").

It is the markets, the stock exchanges, the trading plat-forms, and the regulatory systems. It is an entire ecosystem of people, capital, regulations and technology. This has resulted in mega-trend #4 - a banking and financial eco-system that is moving large amounts of capital through-out China with increasing efficiency and sophistication. It is a very big economic force. Whether it is stable or not is a separate question.

There is an elephant in the room here. And that is the fundamentally political nature of Chinese banking and finance.

The 6 China Megatrends

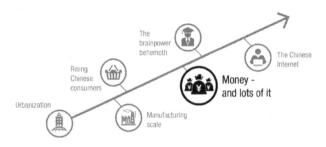

Ask a question like "who controls the Bank of China?" This should be a simple question to answer. Bank of China is, after all, publicly traded. It is certainly run like a banking corporation. And we know who the managers and shareholders are.

However, it turns out the CEO does not really report to the shareholders and is not actually appointed by them. He is chosen by the Organization Department of the Communist Party, which technically owns nothing.

But the CEO also holds a Vice Ministerial rank in the government, which makes Bank of China somewhat of a government ministry as well. But it's also a public company and is traded internationally out of Hong Kong. The key decision-maker seems to be wearing multiple hats here. Suddenly, a basic question like who controls a major Chinese bank is not totally clear. Who controls it on a daily basis? What about over the long-term? What about in a crisis?

Another example: How many loans has the Agricultural Bank of China (ABC) actually made?

It turns out ABC's balance sheet is pretty opaque, which is not uncommon for large banks. But even if you can figure out what the loans are, is that the same thing as actually being owed? Is this something you can sue or collect based on? Loans to state-owned Chinese entities tend to float from SOE balance sheet to SOE balance sheet. And from SOE balance sheet to SOE bank balance sheet. And increasingly to trust company balance sheets. And sometimes they just move off balance sheet into a limbo. "Who owes what" versus "who controls what" versus "who pays what" is not that clear.

Contracts, regulations and terms, which are the mechanics of banking and finance, are frequently rewritten and inconsistently enforced - mostly by political actors. And that makes this all pretty confusing and inscrutable. Chinese financial services is where high finance, state capitalism, and one-party rule all coincide in a great churning mass. Think realpolitik meets really big money. Or what would happen if the Soviet Union and Wall Street had a baby.

There are some interesting developments happening in this right now and there is increasing competition from private and internet banks. But political finance is still the dominant part of the system.

THE STORY OF THE RISE AND RISE OF PING AN

Our short story for Chinese finance is the fairly awesome rise of Peter Ma and Ping An. This is a good example of the scale and increasing sophistication of Chinese finance.

From its launch as a start-up in 1988, Ping An has become a massive Chinese insurance and financial services company with 275,000 staff, 870,000 sales agents, over $100 billion in revenue and 110 million customers (2015). In 2015, net profit exceeded $9 billion, and total assets reached $692 billion. In Dec 2016, the market value of the group exceeded $93 billion. It is now worth more than Prudential, AIG and MetLife. The story of its rise under the leadership of Peter Ma is one of the great China business stories.

Ping An Chairman and CEO Peter Ma (Photo: Imaginechina)

Ping An is also a good example of the tangled nature of Chinese financial services. In under two decades, Ping An has morphed from an insurer to a financial conglomerate that includes banking, asset management, securities, consumer finance and increasingly healthcare. It is a microcosm of the intertwined, constantly shifting, and politically-infused nature of Chinese finance.

Like Wang Shi of China Vanke and Ren Zhengfei of Huawei, the story of Peter (Mingzhe) Ma and Ping An centers on Shenzhen. But if Shi's story is one of urbanization and frantic deal-making and Zhengfei's story is one manufacturing and technology, Peter's story is one of aggressively riding the massive wave of China's financial needs.

Born in 1955, Peter came of age at the same time as Shi and Zhengfei. As a youth, he was one of the "zhiqing", those young people who left the urban areas to work in rural jobs. His early years are a bit unknown, but it is rumored that his father was head of the Shenzhen police and that Peter started on a farm. And definitely, like Shi and Zhengfei, Peter was in Shenzhen at the right time.

In 1988, after working at China Merchants Group, Peter made the decision to found Ping An. He began in a small office in Shenzhen with just a few people. However, the company did receive early funding by two subsidiaries of China Merchants Group and ICBC (each holding 49% and 51% of the shares).

And unlike China Vanke and Huawei, Ping An began not in Shenzhen proper, but in the Shekou Industrial Zone about 30 minutes to the West. The Shekou Industrial Zone, with its deep water port (Shekou means "snake mouth"), gave Shenzhen its dual role as both a financial and shipping doorway to the world. This is the same dual finance and shipping situation seen in cities like New York, Hong Kong – and now in Shanghai's Pudong district.

Ping An Insurance grew rapidly and we are omitting most of the details. On the surface, it was a fairly basic insurance company offering fairly standard insurance products: mainly life insurance, auto insurance (very little of this though – lots of fraud in the market), and so on.

But below the surface, it was one of the most aggressively managed groups in China – particularly in comparison to its mostly state-owned competitors. Over more than 20 years, Ping An grew into the second largest insurance company in the PRC. And along the way, it was the first company to offer individual life insurance in China; the first to appoint international auditors and actuaries; the first to introduce foreign capital; the first to introduce an 'audit – claim' system, as well as the first financial company to hire an international management consulting firm (McKinsey).

It's an impressive story. They were in the right place at the right time for the banking mega-trend. But what makes the Ping An story particularly compelling is two things.

The first is the leadership style of Peter Ma and how he integrated a deeply Chinese organization with Western financial expertise. Even today, Ping An is a traditional Chinese bureaucracy. Across the company, there is the daily ritual of singing the company song and bowing to team leaders before their speeches in the morning.

But at the same time, Peter was arguably one of the most aggressive Chinese CEOs in terms of engaging Western partners and expertise. There are two bronze statues in front of Ping An's university, one of Confucius and the other of Einstein – symbolizing the mix of Chinese and Western expertise.

The second thing that makes Ping An's story compelling is its ambitious growth into other financial sectors. For example:

- After becoming successful in insurance, Ping An set its sights on becoming a national bank. However, in 2003, insurance companies were not permitted to invest in banks. So Ping An indirectly purchased, through its subsidiary Ping An Trust, a 50 percent share of Fujian Asia Bank Ltd (a joint venture bank owned by Bank of China and BCA Finance Limited). They later bought Shenzhen Commercial Bank and consolidated the two bank subsidiaries, resulting in Ping An Bank. Finally in 2010, Ping An successfully completed a strategic investment in Shenzhen Development Bank, beating its competitor China Life Insurance Company. This was how Ping An Insurance became a very large bank.

- Ping An also moved into the trust business, which recently overtook the insurance sector in assets under management. By the end of 2011, Ping An was the largest trust business in China. Ping An Trust is currently invested in by more than 37,000 high net-worth customers.

So today Ping An is actually a trust company, a bank and a brokerage – in addition to an insurance business. It is also number 41 on the Fortune Global 500 list. They are currently building a new corporate headquarters in Shenzhen that will be the world's fourth tallest building when completed.

***

Ok. That is our story for this chapter. This topic is admittedly a bit dry. If you are trying to keep this to one hour, feel free to just read the headlines below.

KEY POINT #1: THE BIG 4 STATE-OWNED BANKS STILL RULE (MOSTLY)

China's big four state-owned banks have traditionally dominated the banking sector. This is still mostly true – although it has changed in the last couple of years. But when in doubt, just watch the big four banks. That will usually get you close to the right answer. In the last few years, money has shifted into shadow banking, trusts and so-called local government financing vehicles, but this has been short-term in nature and the big banks still dominate the system.

The big four banks are the Bank of China, the Industrial and Commercial Bank of China, China Construction Bank and the Agricultural Bank of China. Similar to COFCO, they mostly evolved from government organizations into quasi-corporate, state-owned entities. They benefit from both legacy assets and government connections - and they operate with a mix of commercial and government objectives.

If you are ever on the historic Bund in Shanghai, look for three prominent buildings in a row, just north of the Peace Hotel. Three of the big four banks now have their own buildings on the Bund and, curiously, the buildings decrease in position and physical size in about the same proportion as their political and economic standing in China (shown below).

Three of the big four banks on the Bund - in decreasing stature and size. From the left are the Peace Hotel, Bank of China, ICBC and Agricultural Bank of China (photo by Matt Boulton, Creative Commons license with commercial use)

The big four banks all have big bank financials and we are not going to bore you with them. They have hundreds of billions of assets and liabilities, hundreds of millions of customers, hundreds of thousands of employees, and so on. ICBC is usually ranked as the world's largest bank by market capitalization.

What is important is the way they can, at times, function as an arm of the government into the economy. When the central government wants to influence various aspects of the Chinese economy, directing the lending of the big four banks is a direct tool. They can increase lending to state-owned enterprises and local governments. They can increase lending into infrastructure and strategic industries. They can increase lending across the board to stimulate the economy as a whole. These banks are unique creatures of the China economy.

This also gives these banks a sort of multiple personality disorder. At certain times, they act mostly like commercial banks. Loans are made by loan officers based on economic criteria. At other times, they act like government officials. Loans are made based on government considerations and with less concern for financial viability. This is a big simplification but you can see these two personalities over the past 15 years. You can also see this in their non-performing loan ratios which rise and fall with the dominant personality. Currently, the ratios are rising as the government keeps trying to stimulate the economy with credit.

KEY POINT #2: MOST BIG FOUR BANK LENDING GOES TO BIG SOES AND LOCAL GOVERNMENTS

Big four bank lending tends to go to big state-owned enterprises (SOEs) and local governments. And not to small and medium enterprises (SMEs). While SMEs employ about 80% of the Chinese work force, they account for only 20 percent of bank lending. This creates a serious mismatch and is driving a surge in the shadow banking system (discussed in the next section).

Additionally, SOEs get bank loans for around one-third of the cost of loans to small private companies. This has a lot to do with the difficulty in assessing the risks of private companies in China, particularly SMEs. This follows from underdeveloped credit agencies, less stringent accounting standards, and a lack of expertise and incentives in the banks.

Besides large SOEs, bank credit is also being channeled to local governments. Local infrastructure projects are critical to the development of underdeveloped areas, yet generally have high risks and low returns. Non-state-owned banks won't likely support such projects and small banks don't have the capital to sustain them. So the big state banks are the major supporters.

KEY POINT #3: A SHADOW BANKING SYSTEM HAS EMERGED

In 2003, bank lending accounted for more than 90 percent of Chinese finance. But by 2012, it had dropped to only 50 percent. A large lending market outside the formal banking system had emerged. Part of this is the now frequently discussed shadow banking system.

Shadow banking includes products like wealth management products (WMPs), underground finance and off-balance sheet lending. Wealth management products and trusts pool investors' money and invest them into various projects. However, most of the WMPs do not specify where the funds are used. And one can safely conclude that investors are frequently unaware of the specific risks they are taking with these products.

In comparison with WMPs, trust assets are much more transparent. The trust sector, of which Ping An is the market leader, is considered shadow banking because they are legally non-deposit taking financial institutions. They are not subject to interest rate controls or reserve requirements and can offer higher yields than bank deposits. Infrastructure and real estate can account for over one-third of trust assets. Local government debt is increasingly included in these trust assets, which is why trusts may be dependent on local governments' financial positions.

All of this is pretty confusing. Basically what is occurring is that the big banks are not meeting lending needs. So other non-banking institutions have emerged to supply loans to these customers. Additionally, the big banks are not offering enough investment opportunities. So non-bank lending institutions, also referred to as shadow banks, are filling that gap as well.

But it is the magnitude of Chinese shadow banking that should catch your attention. Fitch ratings estimated that the WMP market was worth over $2.3 trillion at the end of 2012. And assets under management in trusts had reached $1.03 trillion. This was around one-third of Chinese GDP.

KEY POINT #4: SHADOW BANKING WILL INCREASE VOLATILITY

WMPs tend to include investments in long-term real estate projects. However, WMP products tend to have short maturities (1-3 years) so there is a real risk of a mismatch in the maturities of these products. You have a situation similar to the US credit squeeze of 2008 when many investment banks were reliant on an overnight lending market that suddenly dried up.

Additionally, much of the WMP lending is off balance sheet. These are products issued by a third party where the bank acts as an intermediary. The principal of these products is not guaranteed by the bank and thus held off their balance sheet. Investors usually underestimate the risks in these securities because they falsely believe they are bank-backed securities.

Basically, you can find risks like these across the entire shadow banking system. It is essentially chaos. There are risks everywhere. Not just to investors but also to the entire financial system. And there is the feeling that nobody really knows what is going on.

The image that comes to mind is Kowloon's famous Walled City (shown below). Prior to its demolition, it was a bizarre city that ending up existing outside of any real governance, much like shadow banking. And it evolved into a chaotic web of life, business, and illegal dealings.

Kowloon's Walled City was a 6.5-acre settlement located across the water from Hong Kong island. In an arbitrary twist of fate, it was excluded from the 1898 agreement for the Hong Kong territories. This historical anomaly placed the settlement outside of British authority and effectively left it with no government oversight.

Its evolution from that point is a fascinating case study in ungoverned markets and life. It became a lawless city and physically grew into a dense three-dimensional maze. Homes and businesses were built at will. Sewage ran down the sides of buildings and children would jump from rooftop to rooftop. It became a chaotic interconnected mix of homes, schools, businesses, triads, brothels, gambling parlors, and opium dens. By the 1980s, it had the highest human density on the planet. It contained approximately 33,000 families and businesses in more than 300 interconnected high-rise buildings. It was eventually demolished in 1992 by the Hong Kong government.

That's a good image for China's shadow banking system today, which similarly exists outside of any real governance. It has become an interconnected mass of legal and illegal activities. It contains everything from WMPs to individual families making private loans. And to a large degree, nobody really knows what is going on. In Wenzhou for example, it was discovered that over 90 percent of households were involved in lending and shadow banking activities.

This situation not only creates risks. It also affects the dynamics of the Chinese banking sector. There are basically two financial systems competing against each other: the banking sector and shadow banking. Banking is dominated by government regulation while shadow banking is not. This is why, at this moment, shadow banking can sometimes enjoy a competitive edge relative to traditional banking. The CBRC listed shadow banking as one of the three major risks in the banking industry today.

KEY POINT #5: CHINESE DEBT HAS SKYROCKETED IN RECENT YEARS

As mentioned, the Chinese banking system has alternated between its government and commercial personalities. At the most basic level, it is the decision of whether to give a loan or not. Is the decision based on the credit worthiness of the applicant or project - or something else?

In the 1990's, under the direction of Premier Zhu Rong-ji, Chinese banks moved dramatically towards becoming commercial enterprises. Their operations were upgraded. Credit analysis was introduced. Commercial objectives and measurements were introduced. And eventually their legacy of NPLs was cleaned up (or at least moved off balance sheet). They went public as commercial banks, albeit with state owners, in 2005-2006.

In the past several years however, we have seen a sharp reversal of this situation. The other personality has re-emerged in a major way. In response to the financial crisis, the major banks switched to development and stimulus-based loan activities. And the loans came pouring out.

In terms of borrowing, local governments led the charge. And as local governments are mostly not permitted to borrow directly (except for pilot local government bond programs in certain provinces), they often borrow through local government financing vehicles (LGFV). These are separate structures, more than 80 percent of which are from bank loans and more than 50 percent of which are invested in highways and municipal infrastructure projects. So it's really just local governments borrowing indirectly from state banks. The stimulus plan resulted in massive debt creation in these local government vehicles.

This raises the question of how much debt does China actually have? Public and private debt has likely exploded to more than 200 percent of GDP since 2008. It's not really that clear. But everyone thinks it's huge.

FINAL POINT: THERE IS LOTS OF CASH - BUT STABILITY IS A SERIOUS QUESTION

This brings us back to our main point. Which is that there is just a ton of money in China today. And this money is moving freely and with increasing efficiency and sophistication. The financial architecture is in place and is fairly impressive. And the architecture being continually developed is uniquely Chinese. After the recent mostly-Western financial crisis, China feels less compelled to either copy or integrate with the current global system.

We invited Cheah Cheng Hye, founder of Hong Kong-based Value Partners and the "Warren Buffett of Asia", to speak to our students a few years back. During his talk, he made a memorable comment that perhaps the most important challenge for China over the next twenty years is to modernize its system of capital allocation. He mentioned that China has built a national financial system but now needs to modernize it, similar to the modernization of the manufacturing sector over the past twenty years.

As we stated in the Introduction, these mega-trends are not necessarily stable or good things. We only said they are powerful and changing things on the ground. The financial mega-trend is the trend with the greatest likelihood of volatility and potential problems going forward.

Why China is increasingly the world's creditor
© Maxx-Studio /Shutterstock

MEGA-TREND #5: THE BRAINPOWER BEHEMOTH

There is a great story about Steve Jobs freaking out about six weeks before the first iPhone was released. It was reported by *The New York Times* and has become part of the folklore of Steve Jobs. The story goes that about a month before the iPhone release, he summoned his senior team and told them that the iPhone needed a glass screen. The plastic screens on the prototypes were too easily scratched. He wanted an un-scratchable glass screen. And he needed it redone before production started in 4-5 weeks.

The problem was nobody actually knew how to make glass screens for phones at that time.

According to the story, one of Jobs' executives left the meeting and immediately booked a flight to Shenzhen. Their manufacturing partner Foxconn already had over 200,000 workers in Shenzhen ready to assemble the iPhones. And the Shenzhen region has a huge number of engineers, technical experts and specialized companies to draw on for this type of problem. The problem wasn't really cost. The problem was figuring out how to precision cut and grind hardened glass for phones. And how to do it in just a few weeks.

Within days of the executive arriving in China, he received a local bid for the glass work. And he was surprised to find that the Chinese company making the bid had already started arranging a new facility for the project - just in case they got the contract. Their Chinese engineers had already moved into the facility and had started experimenting with glass (reportedly provided by the local government).

The company got the contract and teams began working 24/7 experimenting on the glass. Within four weeks, they had figured it out. The first glass screens were cut, ground and shipped out to Foxconn where they arrived in the middle of the night. Within 2 days, 10,000 glass screen iPhones were coming off the production lines.

Altogether, 200,000 Chinese workers were involved in the production of the first iPhone. And they were overseen by 8,700 Chinese industrial engineers.

There are two important aspects to this story – which may have become somewhat embellished over time. The first is how incredibly fast, flexible, and smart the Chinese manufacturing ecosystem is. This situation was not about being cheap. It was about speed and flexibility. Figuring out how to redesign iPhone screens took lots of brainpower deployed quickly. In the US, the iPhone screens simply could not have been redesigned in such a short timeframe.

The second is that Apple had 8,700 Chinese industrial engineers overseeing production. That is a lot of engineers. The *New York Times* reported that Apple had estimated it would take 9 months to find this many engineers in the US. In China, they found them in about 15 days.

This is a story of Chinese brainpower as a game-changer in global business. The ability to mobilize so much talent, so many engineers, and so quickly, is something new in the world.

But we have also heard this kind of story before.

Twenty years ago, the scale of Chinese manufacturing began emerging as a similarly game-changing phenomenon. Suddenly, everything from shoes to bicycles began to become much cheaper than before. Low-cost Chinese manufacturing changed what was possible in industry after industry. "Made in China" became a household phrase.

Businesses around the world have since incorporated the large-scale and low-cost of Chinese manufacturing into their operations. And it wasn't really optional. Businesses either had to take advantage of the phenomenon or suffer as their competitors did.

The large scale and low cost of Chinese brainpower is another game changer. Suddenly thousands of engineers can be ramped up in a matter of days. And this phenomenon is starting to ripple through industry after industry. What is the impact on the pharmaceutical industry if companies can now access tens of thousands of scientists cheaply? If your competitor is opening a research and development center in China with 10,000 technical specialists, how big of a problem is that for you? Chinese brainpower is starting to impact many industries – often in unexpected ways.

In 2015, there were 7.5M Chinese college graduates (photo: Imaginechina)

KEY POINT #1: THE CHINESE EDUCATION NUMBERS ARE REALLY IMPRESSIVE

The common stereotype of China is that it is a limitless pool of factory workers who will work long hours for low wages. The idea is that China is, more or less, a copy of the Asian tiger export model that was so successful in Thailand, Korea and other markets. China is just a lot bigger.

But in the past ten years, the Chinese government has been very focused on developing skilled human capital on an unprecedented scale. Since 1998, the percentage of GDP dedicated to education has increased by 2-3x. The number of colleges has effectively doubled. And the number of college graduates has gone from approximately 1 million in 1998 to 7.5 million in 2015.

Former Yale President Richard C. Levin has said, "This expansion in capacity is without precedent. China has built the largest higher-education sector in the world in merely a decade's time. In fact, the increase in China's postsecondary enrollment since the turn of the millennium exceeds the total postsecondary enrollment in the United States."

The numbers are impressive. But education is about both quantity and quality. We will discuss the quality problems in later sections. But overall, China's brainpower behemoth is a mega-trend that is becoming more and more important in global business.

The 6 China Megatrends

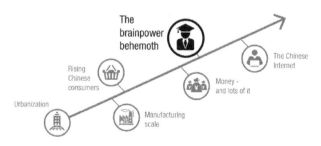

But first a story.

THE RISE AND FALL OF SUNTECH

Suntech Power is a Chinese technology company that went from start-up to global leader in about 6 years. And they did it in a leading-edge technology, solar cells. That was fairly shocking, especially to the dominant Western companies they dethroned. Sure, Chinese companies can make cheap toys but doesn't the West lead in technology? And wasn't green energy technology supposed to be a sector where Western companies had advantages.

It's an important story. It is the story of what happens when you augment large scale, low cost Chinese manufacturing with China's increasing brainpower – and then add in some government support. The results were spectacular.

At its height, Suntech had approximately 15,000 employees and was the world's largest solar panel manufacturer by revenue and volume. It had over $3.4 billion in revenue and 13 offices worldwide. In 2011, it reached a record 2 gigawatts in annual solar cell production. The MIT Technology Review listed Suntech as one of the world's 50 most innovative companies. Fast Company named Suntech as one of the top 10 most innovative companies in China. And Time Magazine listed then CEO Shi Zhengrong as one of its Heroes of the Environment.

In 2012, solar generated over 8 Gigawatts of power in China—in spite of fairly polluted skies
© Pedro Antonio Salaverría Calahorra/123RF Stock Photo

As the solar industry declined in 2009-2012, Suntech was particularly hard hit. And the fairly bad economics of the industry, especially for Chinese solar manufacturers, was exposed. There was way too much manufacturing capacity, margins were razor thin, companies had significant debts and the whole industry depended on Western and Chinese government subsidies that were disappearing. Suntech's revenue declined 48% between 2011 and 2012. In 2013, founder Dr. Shi was removed as CEO and Suntech Power (the main Chinese subsidiary) filed for bankruptcy. *The New York Times* aptly labeled Suntech the "Icarus of the solar power industry".

As we have said, we are focused on mega-trends that fuel business activity. These are the big forces. It doesn't mean people won't behave irrationally. It doesn't mean things will work out well. In fact, you see bubbles, booms and busts in every one of the mega-trends. What is important about Suntech is how they powerfully combined increasing Chinese brainpower with low-cost manufacturing.

A WUXI RAGS TO RICHES STORY

The man behind the Suntech story is Dr. Shi Zhengrong. And his story is quite different than those of Wang Shi, Ren Zhengfei and Peter Ma. He was of the next generation, coming of age in the early 1990s. His career path was one of advanced technical expertise and foreign training. And his launch to billionaire status came from technology in Wuxi. This is a very different story than those who made their riches in Shenzhen's boomtown days.

However his beginnings were arguably the most humble of those we have talked about. He was born in 1963 in a poor farming community on Yangzhong Island, a small island in the Yangtze River about halfway between Nanjing and Shanghai. His parents, suffering through a famine and already raising two other children, gave Zhengrong up for adoption.

Zhengrong's adoptive parents supported him and he is reported to have excelled at school. From there, he went on to Changchun University of Science and Technology in Manchuria and later completed his Master's degree from the Chinese Academy of Sciences. Following the now common path for top Chinese students, he went abroad for graduate work and in 1989 arrived in Australia as a foreign exchange scholar. He eventually earned a doctorate from the University of New South Wales in photovoltaic and solar-electric technologies. The now titled Dr. Shi would eventually receive 11 patents in solar-electric technology.

Suntech Founder Shi Zhengrong (photo: Imaginechina)

The contrast between Dr. Shi's early career and those of Wang Shi, Ren Zhengfei and Peter Ma is stark. Coming of age in the 80s and 90s instead of the 60s and 70s was very much arriving in a different world. His path from China to Western graduate school and then back to China is now a very common one for top Chinese students. A key question Chinese graduate students and professionals working abroad often face is "are you going back to China?" In China, they are referred to as "sea turtles", after animals that return home after a long journey.

In 2001, Dr. Shi made the crucial decision to leave his academic post in Australia and return to China to start a solar energy company. This company would become Suntech.

Timing matters. These were the early days of solar, especially in China. His approach was to take his own technology and expertise and mass produce it. Basically to leverage his technical expertise into China's massive manufacturing scale. He has said that his first goal was to drop the cost of a solar panel from $5 per Watt to $3 per Watt. When he presented this idea to Chinese government officials, he was told that if he could do that the entire Chinese market would be his. He accomplished his goal within the first year of operations.

He also decided to set up operations in Wuxi. This would also prove to be crucial to his success. Wuxi, a city of 4.5 million people located a short train ride from Shanghai, would eventually become the epicenter of solar manufacturing. Long gone were the days when everyone went to Shenzhen. Wuxi had infrastructure, a local critical mass of technical workers and favorable government policies. He was able to tap into significant government support, in particular $6 million in backing from Wuxi government entities.

Suntech began developing and producing solar module products for commercial application. However, what distinguished Suntech from other Chinese solar companies was its emphasis on state-of-the-art innovations and sales to Western markets. The goal was to compete head-to-head with the smartest Western companies in their own markets. And the winning formula for Suntech, and many other Chinese solar companies, would turn out to be combining low-cost manufacturing scale with technical expertise and government support. For better or worse, Suntech did this on a bigger scale than anyone else.

The company grew rapidly. Having only been founded in 2001, it went public on the New York Stock Exchange in 2005. Suntech aggressively expanded its manufacturing capacity. And in 2006, just five years after returning from Australia, Dr. Shi became the richest person in China.

At its peak, Suntech was the market leader in China and the West - having dethroned Western solar players in their home markets and in a field that was a high priority for Western governments. That was a sobering event for many. As mentioned, the solar industry subsequently declined as competitors swamped the market and government subsidies (both in the West and in China) were withdrawn.

There are important lessons in Suntech's rise and fall. The first is how powerful the combination of government support, brainpower and manufacturing is. This is shown on our main chart as three separate mega-trends. The second is how rapidly competition emerged. As Suntech rode a mega-trend to billionaire status, other Chinese companies quickly jumped in. The fierce price war between them (many were selling below cost) had a lot to do with small margins, big borrowing, and government fueled overcapacity. As mentioned in the manufacturing chapter, there is often a last man standing strategy in these fights.

KEY POINT #2: COST INNOVATION IS THE FIRST MANIFESTATION OF CHINA'S BRAINPOWER BEHEMOTH

As soon as the subject of Chinese brainpower comes up, someone inevitably makes a comment about Chinese being good "rote learners" but Westerners are more creative. This is mostly wishful thinking, with a bit of racial stereotyping thrown in.

But the creativity and innovation question is important. What we are seeing a lot of in China is second-generation innovation, often called cost innovation. This is the first real manifestation of China's brainpower behemoth. And we are seeing an incredible amount of constomer-based innovation.

Chinese companies have been exceptionally good at making incremental improvements to existing products - and at making them cheaper and cheaper. In their book *Run of The Red Queen*, authors Michael Murphree and Dan Breznitz write that, "China is a wonderful example of how you don't need to have novel product innovation to be innovative."

Such cost innovation is actually key for market expansion in China. Dropping the cost is what enables you to expand from first tier cities like Beijing to third-tier cities where incomes are much lower. For example, when China Mobile began offering lower priced mobile services to rural areas, they increased their subscriber base by +100 million in approximately 18 months. Getting cheaper is often how you grow in Mainland China. It's how you access more of the domestic market.

As discussed, cost innovation is also a powerful strategy for winning in some foreign markets. Professor Peter Williamson of Cambridge University's Judge School of Business and Ming Zeng of Alibaba make this point in their excellent book *Dragons at Your Door*. They detail several cost-based strategies Chinese companies have used to break into foreign markets. One example is targeting Western specialty manufacturers with low cost Chinese products. For example, targeting high priced refrigerators for wines with lower cost Chinese versions. Niche manufacturers with smaller scale tend to be dependent on higher prices to survive. So they are particularly vulnerable to low cost competition.

Our point is that cost innovation is the first real manifestation of Chinese brainpower. Breznitz and Murphree write, "China's accomplishment has been to master the art of thriving in second-generation innovation—including the mixing of established technologies and products in order to come up with new solutions."

KEY POINT #3: THE R&D WAVE IS THE SECOND MANIFESTATION OF CHINA'S BRAINPOWER BEHEMOTH

In 1993, China accounted for only 2.2 percent of the world's research and development (R&D) investment. By 2009, it had reached 12.8 percent, which placed China well ahead of France, England and most European countries. In 2011, China surpassed Japan (always big news in China) and is now second only to the USA in R&D investment. This is a reflection of Chinese and multinational companies increasingly tapping into China's increasing brainpower.

According to China's Ministry of Commerce, by mid-2012, 490 of the Fortune 500 companies had some presence in China, and over 1,600 R&D centers and regional headquarters had been opened. If you ask a top architecture firm in Shanghai what their biggest business is right now, they will probably say designing new R&D centers. China R&D is a big wave at the moment.

The question is what are these R&D centers actually doing? They're opening big facilities in technology parks. They're hiring engineers and technical specialists. But what are they actually doing?

Our experience is that most of the R&D activity by multinationals in China today is about product localization. It's about adapting products and services to changing Chinese market demands. It's about being close to the customers. And then there is also some basic research and product testing. For example, companies like Broadband have mid-level engineers testing various configurations of electronics for problems.

One example is Anglo–Dutch multinational Unilever, which has over 400 branded consumer products including Dove, Toni & Guy and Ben & Jerry's. They have had a strategic R&D center in Shanghai since 2009 and are reported to have 450 employees working on product development and basic research.

Another example is pharmaceutical giant Merck & Co., which plans to invest $1.5 billion in China and has R&D centers in Shanghai and Beijing. This is in spite of concerns about intellectual property protections. While the company previously conducted only some of its research in China, in the future approximately 600 scientists will perform all stages of drug development there (from basic research to clinical trials).

A counter example is Volkswagen. VW was the first foreign automaker to enter the Chinese market and currently sells the most cars in China. Much of VW's R&D in China focuses on developing solutions to satisfy Chinese market demands and generating cost innovations for existing products. However, VW continues to conduct most of its basic research outside of China.

KEY POINT #4: MANUFACTURING PLUS R&D IS THE WINNING FORMULA

Looking at the combination of Chinese manufacturing (mega-trend #2) and R&D (mega-trend #5), the person who comes to mind is Thomas Edison. While viewed historically as an inventor (he had over 1,000 patents), Edison sat strategically at the intersection of invention and mass production. He was in many ways the architect of the industrialization of the process of invention. And he is credited with the creation of the first industrial research laboratory.

The large manufacturing giants of China today are finding themselves at the same strategic intersection. They have massive manufacturing scale, as discussed in previous chapters. And they increasingly have large numbers of engineers and other highly skilled professionals to draw upon. Like Edison, they are effectively building industrial research laboratories that complement their manufacturing platforms. So what happens when the world's largest telecommunications manufacturer builds the world's largest telecommunications R&D center?

And keep in mind, many of these Chinese manufacturing giants are cash rich (mega-trend #4). They have the resources to invest in R&D long-term. They are also finding acquiring Western companies a good tactic. For example, Chinese auto-parts manufacturer Wanxiang acquired Boston-based lithium battery company A123. This was much to the dismay of Federal officials who had provided A123 with a taxpayer-funded loan.

Back to Huawei and to the question of what happens when the world's largest telco manufacturer builds the world's largest telco research facility.

In 2015, Huawei reported revenue growth of 37 percent to $57 billion and operating profit growth of 33 percent to $6.7 billion. This is a big company with a lot of money. And they are plowing it back into research. The company has a workforce of 170,000 and over 68,000 of them are now in research and development. Compare this to American Cisco, which has 72,000 employees in total.

Huawei has already won as a large scale, low cost telco manufacturer. They are now focused on providing better products and services to their customers, gaining access to new markets, and, most of all, on developing products, not just manufacturing them. The company has research centers in Germany, Sweden, the UK, France, Italy, Russia, India, China, and other countries. They have announced the establishment of 28 joint innovation centers.

This is a winning formula: Chinese manufacturing plus R&D. This is how Huawei is moving from a low-cost manufacturer to a global innovation brand. Not unlike Thomas Edison whose industrial lab eventually became General Electric.

KEY POINT #5: SOME GENERALIZATIONS ABOUT CHINESE BRAINPOWER AND EDUCATION QUALITY

It's hard to talk about Chinese brainpower and the quality of education without making some pretty sweeping generalizations. And generalizations about a country quickly become generalizations about a people. So making generalizations about Chinese education puts us on shaky ground. If something in this section offends, please cut us some slack. However, we are actually professors in China so this is something we know about.

BIG GENERALIZATION #1: THE CHINESE K-12 EDUCATIONAL SYSTEM IS REALLY EFFECTIVE

From birth right up until entering college, the Chinese system is very effective. Sometimes it is too extreme, but nobody can argue that Chinese students are not very highly trained at a young age.

After lunch nap-time in a Hunan primary school (Photo: China Foto Press)

Chinese children often start their formal education at age two. Having tutors and taking extra classes on Saturdays is the norm. Becoming fluent in English is a given. And math and science skills are all far better than in the West. Right up until entering college, the whole system is very effective at developing valuable skills. There is, however, a lot of valid criticism that this system is too demanding.

But this is not just a result of the educational system. It's cultural. It's historical. It's something you see in family after family. Education in China is aggressively sought after and highly respected. Jiang Xueqin, deputy principal of Peking University High School said, "Chinese students love learning. They go to class and they have a real attitude that 'education can change my life.'"

This is, of course, a big generalization. But some generalities are true and this is one of them. Underestimate it at your peril.

And it is important to note that the education system is still a work in progress. Schools and other infrastructure have been deployed very rapidly. As mentioned, universities have doubled in number in the past ten years and things are changing fast. This leads to our second point.

BIG GENERALIZATION #2: THERE IS A MISMATCH BETWEEN UNIVERSITY EDUCATION AND EMPLOYMENT

The quality of most of China's universities remains below Western standards. This is creating a serious problem: significant unemployment amongst university graduates, even as thousands of jobs for graduates go unfilled.

A job fair in Wuhan in 2010 (Photo: China Foto Press)

A 2005 McKinsey study made a comment about China's educational quality that still rings true today:

"Consider engineers. China has 1.6 million young professionals, more than any other country [in the study]. Indeed, 33 percent of the university students in China study engineering, compared with 20 percent in Germany and just 4 percent in India. But...Chinese students get little practical experience in projects or teamwork compared with engineering graduates in Europe or North America...The result of these differences is that China's pool of young engineers considered suitable for work in multinationals is just 160,000—no larger than the United Kingdom's. **Hence the paradox of shortages amid plenty** (bold added)."

BIG GENERALIZATION #3: INTELLECTUAL PROPERTY THEFT IS A BIG PROBLEM IN BRAINPOWER INDUSTRIES

Work based on brainpower quickly leads to a discussion of intellectual property (IP) theft. IP can often follow highly trained employees out the door. And IP theft is everywhere in China. Designs, customer lists, technologies, etc. Foreign and domestic companies across all industries have experienced IP infringement by employees, competitors, clients, joint venture partners and third party service providers.

This is a particularly pernicious problem for cost-intensive and long-term research fields, such as pharmaceuticals and automotive. Both of these factors heavily impact China's image and still hinder foreign companies from fully committing to China as an R&D location.

FINAL POINT: PATENT FILINGS ARE ACTUALLY A GOOD MARKER FOR THE CHINESE EDUCATION SITUATION

In theory, the number of patents filed should track the brainpower of a country. And the number of domestic patent filings in China has grown dramatically.

China filed 37.2 percent of all patents between 1995 and 2009 but 72.1 percent between 2009 and 2011. Between 2008 and 2011, Chinese patent filings increased by 22 percent annually, compared to a world average growth rate of only around 4 percent. Consequently, China is today the world's leading patent filer, followed by the

United States and Japan. On the surface this would seem a pretty good marker of brainpower.

However, just as the number of students in Chinese universities is not an indicator of those schools' quality, the number of patents filed is also not an indicator of quality either. Very few of these patents are at a quality level one would consider comparable to Japan or the West. So, ironically, patent filings - with their surging quantity obscuring problematic quality - do mirror the situation in the Chinese educational system.

However, what the patent filings do show is that the research processes are now in place. People are doing research. People are publishing. And people are getting in the habit of filing patents. And that is how innovation ultimately happens. Millions of people get in the habit of studying, researching and filing patents. The quality follows from this process over time.

***

That is our assessment of China's brainpower behemoth today. The graduates are there. The educational and corporate structures are in place. The research processes are functioning. And the economics driving all of this are powerful (i.e., a mega-trend). So as this continues over time, the quality and innovation should come naturally.

Warren Buffett's partner Charlie Munger may have described this phenomenon the best when he said, "I think they have been lucky that the Communist Party in China evolved into a Confucian meritocracy where everyone's been to engineering school."

China is becoming a curious mix of 21st century brainpower amidst a 20th century industrial economy
(© silverjohn/123RF Stock Photo)

MEGA-TREND #6: THE CHINESE INTERNET

What is distinctive about this final mega-trend is that it is both newer and much, much faster than the others.

The Internet is a recent phenomenon in China. The overall penetration rate is still low at 48 percent, as compared to approximately 85 percent in the USA. And while the total number of Chinese users online is large (668 million in China vs. 287 million in the US in 2016), this has mostly been a phenomenon of just the last few years. Of the 668 million Chinese currently online, the majority of them have been online for under five years. So things are moving at a very rapid pace.

Some of the results of this mega-trend have been predictable. For example, Chinese has already replaced English as the primary language of the Internet. Another is that the money involved has become very large. Chinese retail e-commerce is now the largest in the world. And looking at the chart below, it is shocking how much China has come to dominate the Internet.

Chinese Internet users over time

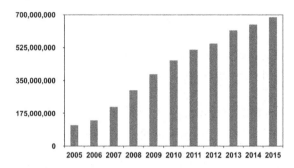

Source: CNNIC

Internet users by country - as of 06/30/2016*

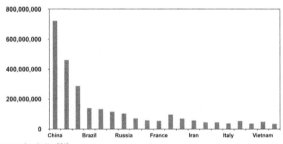

* - Europe numbers by Nov 2015
Source: Internet World Stats,

HOWEVER...

What is really fascinating is how unpredictable the Chinese Internet is. It is a constant source of surprises to everyone from companies to consumers to government officials. It's a bit of frenzy.

Looking back, most people in the US and Europe were introduced incrementally to most online products and services. Facebook followed Google. Google followed Amazon. Hotmail followed regular email. And so on. People gradually shifted aspects of their life online over time. And they discovered these things slowly.

However, in China it happened all at once. People gained instant access to a whole range of online products and services they had never seen before. Videos, music, chat, games, news, dating, shopping, etc. And yes, they went a little bit crazy. People began chatting all day long. People spent huge amounts of time online gaming. And everything from clothes to pens started being purchased online. It's not a coincidence that China was the first country to designate Internet addiction as a disease.

Another interesting aspect is the new China "inter-connectedness". While China has had a common cultural identity for centuries, it has been largely a fragmented and disconnected society. It has been a country of thousands of villages spread across a huge land mass. People in villages in Guangdong historically have not interacted much with people in, say, Qingdao. And most media has been delivered top-down.

However, the Internet is letting people become inter-connected for the first time. Suddenly, people across the country are sharing information, giving shopping tips, dating, expressing opinions, and interacting with each other on a daily basis. We are witnessing the emergence of a real-time "Chinese consciousness." Now, when there is a China-Japan dispute in the South China Sea or a celebrity sex scandal in Hong Kong, the Chinese people have an opinion. Actually, they have many, many opinions. Most of the online forums have only been around for a few years and they are great reading - funny, angry and chaotic. A personal favorite is how Chinese blogs all refer to the North Korean dictator Kim Jong Un as Fatty the Third ("san pang" in Mandarin).

The 6 China Megatrends

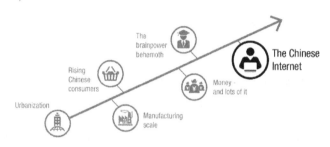

THE STORY OF PONY AND TONY: CHINA'S FIRST INTERNET MOGULS

Our story for this final mega-trend is Tencent Holdings. Today it is one of the top ten Internet companies in the world, typically listed right after Facebook and Amazon. However it remains virtually unknown in the West.

Tencent was originally known for its instant messenger service (QQ) with its cute penguin. It is now most well-known for its WeChat mobile messanging application. There are over 700 million active WeChat accounts, making Tencent one of the world's largest online communities.

But Tencent has expanded from a simple messenger to a very large and lucrative ecosystem of web portals, communication services and online multiplayer games. And Tencent dominates online gaming - not just in China, but also in the US and everywhere else. Think of Tencent in online games the way you would think of Hollywood for movies.

THE RISE OF PONY AND TONY

It all started in Shenzhen in November 1998. Twenty-six year-old Ma Huateng, also known as Pony, and Zhang Zhidong, also known as Tony, launched a simple instant messaging service named OICQ. It was a basic messenger service, very similar to Yahoo Messenger and MSN Messenger. The name was soon simplified to just QQ and a cute penguin was added as the logo.

These were the earliest days of China's Internet. The first commercial networks had been set up only three years earlier. The first Chinese Internet company, China Pages, had just been created (by Jack Ma, later of Alibaba fame). And when Pony and Tony launched their service, there were likely fewer than 20 million people online in all of China. Fortunately, chat and messaging would quickly prove to be China's most popular online activity.

But as we mentioned, most of China's Internet growth did not really happen until the last few years. So even five years after launch, the wildly popular QQ service still had only about 10 million users. Compare that to the hundreds of millions of noodle customers for Master Kong. Or to the billions of dollars spent on China Vanke's apartments. The Chinese internet was a sexy trend that got a lot of attention. But it was actually quite small for a long time.

Tencent went public in Hong Kong in June 2001. And Pony and Tony became China's first Internet moguls. Note: Tencent was founded in November of 1998. That was one month before Jack Ma founded Alibaba in Hangzhou. So technically they were first.

Fast-forward to today and Wechat (and QQ) has exploded to more than 700 million users. For comparison, Skype's audience is 3 times less on a daily basis: just 40 million active users. In 2016, Pony Ma was ranked as China's third-richest person with a net worth of $24 billion.

Tencent Co-Founder and Chairman, Pony Ma (photo: Imaginechina)

THE SECRET OF THEIR SUCCESS

As we mentioned, instant messaging is the one of the most popular online activities in China. But Tencent has actually moved far beyond its popular instant messaging service. They have added software skins, images, motions, chat rooms, games, personal avatars, internet storage, internet dating services, gaming, web portals, and many other services. Their current service offering integrates all of these into an ecosystem that has no real comparable in the West. According to Dean Takahashi of VentureBeat, Tencent is "a little like what you would get if you combined AOL, Facebook, Skype, Yahoo, Gmail, Norton, and Twitter under one roof."

The key is the customer progression within the Tencent ecosystem (note: this is a big simplification).

- Users typically start with Tencent's free WeChat or QQ accounts, which many Chinese teenagers use for chatting and for building and maintaining relationships. These have all the high switching costs we associate with network effects.

- Over time, many users grow addicted to Tencent's free gaming modules within their service. These multi-player online games have proven to be very popular and Tencent ties these to their QQ network.

- Instant messaging, online gaming, web portals, and other services create an online ecosystem for the user to live in online. And the online ecosystem has a very, very large population. That makes it unique.

- Across this ecosystem, Tencent sells low cost virtual items. Users start spending money on in-game purchases, mobile screen skins, and experience points for games. Most services remain free and the fees for the virtual items are tiny. The end result is lots of tiny fees multiplied across a huge volume of activity.

This one-of-a-kind business has made Tencent a financial powerhouse with a market capitalization of over $240 billion (2016). The company enjoys a 61 percent gross profit. Tencent is considered one of the world's most valuable digital franchises.

TENCENT IS NOW INVADING THE WEST

Tencent's strength in messaging and online multiplayer games puts it in a unique position for global expansion. Both of these services cross borders fairly easily. For example, the online game League of Legends (one of the most popular videogames in the world) is pretty much the same in the US and China.

And this is what is happening right now. As Tencent's SEVP David Wallerstein said: "All the major videogame, technology, and media companies in North America and Europe are both fascinated and slightly nervous about the major Chinese companies entering their home markets. The only advice I can give is to learn from Tencent fast, because these guys mean business and they know what they're doing. It is only a matter of time before they become as strong internationally as they are at home." Tencent has, according to Dean Takahashi of Venture-

Beat, "the market power to acquire just about every major video game company in the U.S."

***

That's our last story. But as the Chinese Internet is pretty fascinating, we're going into depth on a couple of key points. Feel free to skim if you're over an hour.

KEY POINT #1: CHINESE SPEND A LOT MORE TIME ONLINE

On average, Chinese Internet users spend 19.9 hours online per week. That is 5-6 more hours online per week than Americans. According to a McKinsey study, the time allocation of a typical Chinese user typically includes:

- 4 hours on chatting and instant messaging, which is 10 times more than in the US

- 3 hours on gaming, much of which includes communication with friends

- 2.5 hours on social media

- Less than 30 minutes emailing versus 5 hours in the US

And many of these activities are not free. A teenager in a province like Guilin can easily spend more than 20 percent of his allowance on online communication ($8 out of $30 monthly).

KEY POINT #2: INTERNET OBSESSION AND ADDICTION ARE REAL PROBLEMS IN CHINA

Internet addiction is a real thing in China, especially in rural areas where there are fewer opportunities for entertainment. Young people often spend hours after school in local Internet cafes, gaming and communicating with their friends. The Chinese government has implemented a rule that requires people under the age of 18 to present their IDs in the cafes and to limit their gaming time to 3 hours per day. Unsurprisingly, young gamers are easily finding ways to circumvent these requirements with fake IDs and other means.

In 2012, there was a funny story about a father who was so exasperated by his 23 year-old son's Internet usage (mostly online gaming) that he hired other players in his son's favorite games to go online and kill off his characters.

KEY POINT #3: CHINESE NETIZENS ARE PROBABLY THE MOST ACTIVE IN THE WORLD

Forrester Research classified 47 percent of the online Chinese population as "creators", meaning they actively create their own content online (blogs, web pages, videos, articles etc.). In comparison, only 21 percent of US Internet users create such online content.

This turns out to be a perfect opportunity for marketers. For example, Master Kong (discussed in the consumer chapter) partnered with Internet company Tudou to create a video-sharing service. They proposed to consumers that they upload videos about their experiences with the company's new jasmine tea. The result was more than 300,000 uploads and more than 3 million views.

KEY POINT #4: ONLINE WORD OF MOUTH IS THE MOST TRUSTED SOURCE OF INFORMATION

After decades of media censorship, it is safe to describe China as a fairly skeptical society. People overwhelmingly don't trust what they read or what they are told. What they do trust, however, are things they were advised of by somebody they know (i.e., word of mouth).

So it is not surprising that this skeptical public has rushed online for news and discussion. And in China, one of the primary destinations has been Weibo - a hybrid of Twitter, Facebook, and online bulletin boards. One reason for this is the Chinese language itself. 140 characters in Chinese can contain up to 5 times as much information as English. The influence of Internet discussions in China is substantially more than in nearly every other part of the world.

ONLINE WORD OF MOUTH IS POWERFUL - IN GOOD AND BAD WAYS

Businesses are well aware of the importance of online word of mouth in China. News and rumors online can have a powerful impact on a product and a business. Rumors can make or break your business.

This turned out to be a pleasant surprise for L'Oreal. Back in 2006 L'Oreal's websites were mainly passive, content filled pages. The company referred to them as "online museums." However, in 2007, a customer in China who liked one of Lancôme's products, Rosebeauty, wrote a poem describing how it "enriched her life and made it more beautiful." To find this woman, Lancôme initiated a campaign called "Who is the Rosebeauty girl?" The results were stunning. More than 100,000 users took part in the program, which at the time was more than the number of registered users at Lancôme's official website. Thousands claimed to be the poem's author. The company eventually identified a woman named Cherry as the author.

What L'Oreal realized was that it could engage with its China customers. And that customers were eager to engage with them. Within three years, Lancôme became the largest commercial cosmetics forum in China with over 100,000 members. Today, Lancôme's beauty community site, Rosebeauty, is one of the largest online beauty forums in the country.

But word of mouth can also be powerfully negative. Criticisms of product quality (especially of food) online can quickly devastate sales. Examples of online discussions impacting business are numerous.

And this is the central problem. Whether a company does or does not engage in social media, the conversations about the company's products will take place anyways. Maybe it will be positive? Maybe it will be negative? Maybe it will be driven by competitors? But it will happen regardless.

Interestingly, the role of bloggers is also much more powerful in China. Mostly because there is less "traditional media" to compete with. According to the Boston Consulting Group, 7 percent of Chinese netizens drive 40 percent of online sales. These social enthusiasts and key opinion leaders (i.e., those who spend the most time on social-media websites) can significantly influence a company's image.

KEY POINT #5: CHINESE E-COMMERCE IS THE NEXT REALLY BIG THING

On November 11th, 2016, Alibaba, the leading Chinese e-commerce company, had its one-day shopping promotion that coincides with China's "double eleven" holiday. This 11/11 event, also called singles' day, is somewhat comparable to America's Cyber-Monday, the online shopping day held after Thanksgiving. But while Cyber-Monday and Black Friday generated a combined $4.5 billion in sales in 2015, Alibaba's one day promotion generated $17.8 billion in 2016. It is the world's largest shopping event by far. At peak volume, Alibaba was registering 175,000 transactions and 120,000 payments per second.

Chinese e-commerce and online (and mobile) payments are the next really big thing. Chinese retail e-commerce has already passed the US in terms of both volume and dollars. And this phenomenon is continuing to grow with increased internet penetration and rising consumer wealth. It's a really big deal and could easily fill an entire chapter.

Arguably the "Steve Jobs of China", Alibaba Founder Jack Ma
(photo: Imaginechina)

FINAL POINT: THE CHINESE INTERNET IS WINNER TAKE ALL - AND CHINESE COMPANIES ARE WILLING TO BET IT ALL

Similar to the West, the Chinese Internet is dominated by a few big companies. The big three are Baidu in search, Tencent in instant messaging and gaming, and Alibaba in e-commerce. For example, in 2015 Baidu ranked as the fourth most visited website in the world, according to the research firm Alexa. Baidu.com is more popular than Amazon.com, Twitter.com, and Wikipedia.org.

However, even though Baidu is the market leader and claims two-thirds of the Chinese search market, other web companies are not afraid to challenge them. That is what is striking about the Chinese Internet. It is a ruthlessly competitive market. In 2012, Qihoo 360, an anti-virus software company also offering a popular Internet browser, entered the Chinese search market and has reportedly been able to gain a ten percent market share.

The key point is that the Chinese Internet is a winner-take-all, ruthless business - and companies are willing to bet it all to win.

So yes, the Chinese Internet is a mega-trend. It is exciting and it can be a huge wealth machine for entrepreneurs. But it is also spectacularly competitive. As mentioned at the start of this chapter, this is a phenomenon that is changing more quickly than any of the others. Every year we have students who get excited about the Chinese Internet and want to do a start-up. Jeff's standard reply is that there are two industries he is terrified of competing in in China. The first is a local restaurants (seriously, check out the 50 page menus and crazy staffing and service levels). The other is Internet companies. It's just too ruthless of a space.

China's version of Fedex (© Karen Struthers/123RFStock Photo)

FINAL THOUGHTS

There has been a significant shift in the media commentary on China. The news stories have all shifted from China as a success story to China as a slowing economy. There has also been an increased focus on China's rising debt – and what that means for the government and the economy. Basically, the overly pessimistic in the press have overtaken the overly optimistic.

We find neither the optimist nor the pessimist case particularly helpful. China is developing so rapidly and on such a vast and complex scale that instability and chaos are a natural part of it. Looking for stable growth (the optimist case) is ridiculous. Being concerned about volatility (the pessimist case) means you don't really know what country you are in. China is experiencing regular booms and busts across its economy the same way a rocket ship experiences turbulence.

Our argument is that there are powerful economic and demographic mega-trends shaping things on the ground – irrespective of booms and busts. These trends are all broad and long term. They are driving most of the daily activity by companies and make things somewhat predictable. Basically, ignore the hype, the pessimists and the optimists. Stay focused on the basics. Business is business. And business in China is spectacular.

The 6 China Megatrends

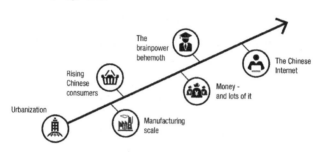

A couple of final comments on our simple chart.

We have placed urbanization as the starting point. It really does cut across most every industry and geography. And it is by far the most important trend in the country.

Urbanization also ties with the manufacturing and money trends we have placed next to it. All three have a lot do with the infrastructure and real estate being deployed across the country.

Above the line, we have placed the more intangible and human capital aspects: consumers and brainpower. And if you take a look at recent China headlines (business, not political), most of what you see are combinations of the six mega-trends.

CHINA IS BIG

Thanks for taking the time to read this. We hope it was useful. If we did our job right, you should be at about 60-80 minutes time spent. Hopefully you got a reasonable return on that investment.

Returning to our original opening point, China is just really big. It's a complicated subject that you really can spend a lifetime studying and struggling with. But we think we've touched on most of the important points. If something in particular caught your interest, there are lots of big, weighty China books on each individual sub-topic.

Also, if you are curious, we have a best-selling follow-up to this book, called the One Hour China Consumer Book. (www.onehourchina.com).

Our thanks for reading and cheers,
Jonathan and Jeff

A final recommendation: Do the river trip in Yangshuo (near Guilin). You can spend the afternoon going down the river on a little raft while having super-soaker water fights with other rafts. And merchants will paddle up to sell you beer and barbecue along the way. It's awesome. (photo: feiyuezhangjie / Shutterstock)

Made in the USA
Monee, IL
30 November 2019

17649608R10085